TWELVE

COUNCIL

FATHERS

TWELVE

COUNCIL

FATHERS

❧ WALTER M. ABBOTT, S.J. ☙

The Macmillan Company, New York
Collier-Macmillan Limited, London

55850

SEP 19 1963

Imprimi potest:
    John V. O'Connor, S.J.
    Provincial
    New England Province
    Boston, Massachusetts
    April 23, 1963

Nihil obstat:
    Edward J. Montano, S.T.D.
    Censor Librorum

BX
830
1962
A53

Imprimatur:
    ✠Francis Cardinal Spellman
    Archbishop of New York
    May 8, 1963

The nihil obstat and imprimatur are official declarations that a book or pamphlet is free of doctrinal or moral error. No implication is contained therein that those who have granted the nihil obstat and imprimatur agree with the contents, opinions or statements expressed.

Chapters II and V originally appeared in full in *America,* as well as much of the material in chapters I, III, IV, VI, IX, XI and XII.

© Walter M. Abbott 1963

First Printing

The Macmillan Company, New York
Collier-Macmillan Canada Ltd., Toronto, Ontario

Library of Congress catalog card number: 63-19434

Printed in the United States of America

DESIGNED BY RONALD FARBER

TO

HIS EMINENCE

RICHARD CARDINAL CUSHING

ARCHBISHOP OF BOSTON

ৰ্চ্চ ৈ্

CONTENTS

[vi]

CONTENTS   [vii]

PREFACE

As the feature editor of *America*, I remained at my desk in New York during the first session of the Second Vatican Council. The editor in chief, Thurston N. Davis, S.J., and our Vatican expert, associate editor Robert A. Graham, S.J., reported from Rome during that session of the Ecumenical Council. Another associate editor, C. J. McNaspy, S.J., attended the closing of the session.

On his return, Father Davis told me he had heard much favorable comment about my interview with Cardinal Léger, the Archbishop of Montreal. That interview had been front-page news in many papers of the United States and Canada when it was published in the May 12, 1962, issue of *America*. Father Davis said he would like to have me go to Europe to interview other leading prelates of the Council, sometime during the period between the sessions, when the cardinals and bishops would have had a chance to clear their desks back home and start thinking again about the future of the Council.

In view of the ecumenical possibilities, the National Conference of Christians and Jews gave me a grant that would take care of my air travel. I wish to thank the Conference for that gracious gift, and the group of *America* benefactors known as America Associates who provided the matching funds that I needed. Cardinal Cushing, Archbishop of Boston, sent a letter to each cardinal on my route in Italy, Austria, Germany and Holland. A letter from Cardinal Léger went to French-speaking

Cardinals Suenens and Liénart. The backing and the confidence of Cardinal Cushing and Cardinal Léger, communicated in those letters to their brothers in the Sacred College, assured me of a cordial reception in every case. Another good friend, Monsignor John E. Steinmueller, of Brooklyn, New York, wrote to his classmate and fellow biblical scholar, the Archbishop of Florence, who received me as graciously as the cardinals did.

In his letter, Cardinal Léger wrote: "I do not have to tell you that *America* is one of the most important Catholic publications, not only on this continent but in the entire world." Cardinal Cushing, in his letter, referred to me as his "lifelong friend." When I met each cardinal, I hastened to explain that I was only forty years old and therefore that His Eminence was referring to my life, not his, when he used the word "lifelong"—he has known me practically all my life. This got the interview off to a good start in each case. I think that, as a result, the interviews were unusually frank and informative. Most of the cardinals accepted my proposal that we talk for an hour or two, and then I would type out the interview, in order that the cardinal could look it over and approve it later that same day. In all these cases, I left the cardinal's house with the fully approved text in my briefcase.

All of the interviews in this book are authentic, historical documents. They are, I believe, of considerable importance, for each Father of the Council took the opportunity to communicate his ideas, on key topics and issues of the Council, knowing that he would reach a large audience of important readers. In a number of cases, those readers may have read something like the ideas expressed by these Council Fathers—in works by modern theologians, Scripture scholars and others active in ecumenical work—but, however objectively possible and desirable many ideas are, they remain largely just so much intellectual delectation unless and until bishops take them up, approve them and promote them. Wherever that is done in this book—and it is done often—the reader will discern the importance of the interview.

In these interviews, cardinals and bishops put life and meaning into certain ideas about the college of bishops, the role of the laity, Church-State questions, changes in Canon Law concerning marriage, the Index of Prohibited Books, etc. I hope the reader will allow me to point out, in view of my special interest in the matter, the significant contribution made by three cardinals to the discussion about a common Bible for Catholics and Protestants.

With the development of modern languages, and the decline of Latin as a common language, it became necessary to have vernacular translations of the Bible, in order that the sacred library of God's word could continue to be the common heritage of people speaking the same language. The Protestant Reformation and its aftermath produced two different traditions of Bible translation and Bible study. In recent times, however, the careful, objective research of Protestant and Catholic scholars has resulted in such agreement about the original languages of the Bible books that there is now a real possibility Protestants and Catholics may soon have, again, a common Bible in the language of the country or region where they live. This was the thesis that I advanced in an article entitled "The Bible Is a Bond," in the October 24, 1959, issue of *America*. Not only was it possible, I argued; it was highly desirable. An objective, accurate translation, worked out by Catholic and Protestant scholars and approved by Church authorities, could put an end to the different numberings of Commandments and Psalms that needlessly confuse and divide us; it would give us uniform spellings of biblical names (an incomparable boon to compilers of atlases, concordances and dictionaries of the Bible as well as the users of them); it would give a great psychological lift to the ecumenical movement by providing Catholics and Protestants engaged in ecumenical dialogue with a vivid awareness of how much they actually have in common. One could ask, in fact, what hope there was for success in the ecumenical movement unless agreement could be reached about the Bible—the books to be accounted as belonging to it, the translation of them, and, finally, the interpretation of them.

The renewed interest of Catholics in the Bible and the interest of the Catholic Church in Christian unity were significantly underlined for Protestant observers by Pope John XXIII when he appointed Augustin Cardinal Bea to be president of the Secretariat for Promoting Christian Unity. It was manifestly a providential choice, for Cardinal Bea is one of the most respected biblical scholars of our times. It was chiefly to Cardinal Bea, obviously, that Catholics and Protestants would communicate their hopes about a common Bible and the desire for consideration of the idea by the Second Vatican Council.

By the time the Council began, there were considerable hopes and desires throughout the world. The idea of the common Bible was a topic of serious discussion among Fathers of the Council and delegate-observers of various churches. Bishop Fred P. Corson, president of the World Methodist Council and an official delegate-observer at Vatican II for his group, declared, on a trip back to Philadelphia during the Council's first session, that one of the results he hoped for from the Fathers was approval for the idea of "one Bible in the vernacular, prepared jointly by Catholic and Protestant scholars." The Protestant Episcopal Bishops of the United States and the House of Deputies had adopted a resolution at their triennial general convention, in Detroit, in September, 1961, expressing the hope that a translation of the Bible could be produced which would be acceptable to all, including Roman Catholics. Anglican, Episcopalian and Methodist bishops we had talked with were looking forward, we knew, like Bishop Corson, to the day when Cardinal Bea would present to the Second Vatican Council that part of his Secretariat's announced agenda which deals with the Bible as a bond of unity. It was then, they hoped, that the Council would consider making a statement about the common Bible.

It heartened interested Protestants and Catholics considerably when Joseph Cardinal Frings, Archbishop of Cologne, announced shortly before the Council opened that he and the bishops of Germany had given Catholic scholars permission to prepare a new translation of the Bible with the help of Protestant scholars.

Cardinal Frings, chairman of the German Bishops' Conference, revealed that the desired goal of this collaboration was to work out a translation at least of the most important parts of the Bible —the Our Father, for example—to be used by both Catholics and Protestants. In recent years Protestant churchmen had been talking more and more about the need for a modern German translation of the Bible. There had been so much discussion, by April, 1962, about the possibility of working this translation out with Catholics that a workshop on Catholic-Protestant relations at the annual conference of the Central Committee of German Catholics recommended a common Bible text for Catholics and Protestants. It was in September, 1962, that Cardinal Frings made his announcement.

In the Netherlands, as Cardinal Alfrink explains in his interview, the Catholic Bible Society of St. Willibrord has already completed a translation of the New Testament with the help of Protestant scholars. That Catholic Bible Society itself had been established with the help of Protestants. Cardinal Alfrink referred explicitly to that fact in February, 1961, when he accepted the foundation deeds of the new society in the presence of the Papal Internuncio and the bishops of Holland. The cardinal stated that the Protestant Bible Society had given help and support to the Catholic organization, and he added: "I rejoice exceedingly that Christians have found each other in the Holy Scriptures. The Bible is always the starting point and the basis of every real meeting." The day I talked with Cardinal Alfrink at his home in Utrecht, I said I had heard that a Catholic bishop in Denmark had given his imprimatur to a Protestant translation of the Bible, which he regarded as sufficiently accurate, instead of commissioning a whole new Catholic translation. "I have done that, too," said Cardinal Alfrink, "in Friesland, for the Book of Psalms." He explained that the language of the people of Friesland was different from both Dutch and German, and they did not have a translation of the Psalms in a Catholic edition. When he decided to give his imprimatur to a Protestant translation of that book, nobody questioned his judgment. The cardinal is one of the great Catholic biblical scholars of Europe. When the Second Vatican Council assembled in October, 1962, there were also some French bishops present who had looked into the question of a common Bible for Catholics and Protestants. In France, a group of Catholic and Protestant scholars had already produced a French translation of St. Luke's Gospel. They had managed to come to final agreement, and they submitted their text for ecclesiastical approval. It was published by Unité Chrétienne, a Catholic organization working in Lyons for Christian unity. From the beginning, with the approval of the Catholic bishops concerned, their purpose had been to bring out a text that could be distributed by Catholic and Protestant colporteurs.

Also very much in evidence at the opening of the Second Vatican Council were Archbishop John Murphy, of Cardiff, Wales, and Bishop John Petit, of Menevia, who had earlier in the year agreed to explore the possibilities of a translation of the Bible into Welsh, to be done by a committee of Catholics and Protestants. The archbishop and the bishop had been assured by Catholic experts that the project was a possibility because there was now such objective, scientific progress in the field of philology on the part of both Protestants and Catholics. Archbishop Murphy said that the work was "well within the vein of the current ecumenical spirit." He added: "With reservations to accommodate Catholic and non-Catholic requirements, the work may proceed." The director of the translation board, the bishops agreed, would be W. R. Williams, principal of the Protestant Theological College at Aberystwyth.

By his reference to "requirements" (as I explained in an article entitled "Bishops and the Common Bible," *America*, December 8, 1962), Archbishop Murphy had in mind the present legislation of the Catholic Church that presentations of the Bible in the vernacular must be accompanied by notes. The nature and number of the notes are not specified by Canon Law. In general, Protestants have long resented this ruling, and some Protestant churches have legislated that their editions of the Bible are to have no footnotes at all. The American Bible Society and its counterparts in other countries have a rule forbidding them to publish translations with notes. It is no secret that a number of bishops have been requested by interested parties to consider changing the Church's present law about the matter. Now that good Catholic commentaries are available to the people, even in low-priced pamphlet form, the possibility of dropping the requirement for footnotes is more likely to be considered.

Archbishop Murphy's willingness to enter into negotiations about a common Bible encouraged the Anglican Archbishop of Wales, Dr. Edwin Morris, to say: "This is one thing on which we can cooperate, although it will mean working in cooperation for a long time. Let us hope it will work out all right. It will mean about ten years of hard work."

In England, Archbishop John C. Heenan, of Liverpool, had let it be known that he would be willing to adopt the New English Bible as his official New Testament. (Only the New Testament part of that project, sponsored by Protestant churches of Great Britain, had appeared; the Old Testament was still to be finished.) As long ago as December, 1960, the editor in chief of the Catholic paper in Cape Town, South Africa, encouraged by news of common Bible thinking overseas, had suggested in an editorial that the possibility be explored of an "arrangement by which the existing non-Catholic translations in African languages could be made acceptable to Catholics." He was thinking especially of the work Protestants have done on translations into Zulu, Xhosa, Sesotho and Afrikaans—major languages of his region in which no Catholic Bible has appeared. There are Catholic translations of the New Testament in English, Zulu and Sesotho, languages spoken by about 85 percent of the Catholics in South Africa, but by only 40 percent of the total population. However, the only Catholic translation of the Old Testament available to Catholics in the southern part of Africa is in English, and English is the language of only about 12 percent of the Catholics and 10 percent of the whole population. These facts indicate why African bishops are known to be studying the common Bible idea and thinking about using the latest objective results of Protestant scholarship in some of the new Protestant translations of the Bible. Some bishops in Asia are looking into the matter for similar reasons.

In the United States, shortly before the first session of the Council began, Bishop John J. Wright, of Pittsburgh, said, in an interview during the National Catholic Laymen's Retreat Conference held at Portland, Oregon: "A common Bible for Protestants and Catholics is very possible." He added that agreement on a common Bible would create a means of exploring the roots of the Christian tradition harmoniously, in contrast with the past practice of using the Bible in a polemical or defensive manner. Bishop John J. Dougherty, president of Seton Hall University and one of America's best-known biblical scholars, had already spoken favorably about the common Bible idea before he was elevated to the episcopacy. After the first session of the Ecumenical Council, several American bishops made public statements in favor of the common Bible idea, e.g., Archbishop John P. Cody, of New Orleans ("I hope such a Bible will be one of the great results of the Council") and Auxiliary Bishop Philip M. Hannan, of Washington, D.C., who told the John Carroll Society that he predicted the Council would open the way for the publication of one Bible for all Christians.

When Cardinal Bea came to Harvard University's four-day Protestant-Catholic colloquium, he said, in the first of his three lectures: "Holy Scripture is the common ground of all Christians. If all who believe in Christ will read the Scriptures in prayerful meditation and incorporate its teaching into their lives, they will not only be drawn closer to Christ, but inevitably closer to one another. This penetration into the spirit of Christ which brings together human hearts and minds will aid us enormously in reaching objective interpretation of those texts which are presently the subject of divergent interpretations." It was on the day after that speech that I interviewed Cardinal Cushing. He gave me then the important statement about the common Bible which is contained in that remarkable interview.

In addition to the statements of Cardinal Alfrink and Cardinal Cushing in this book, there is, of course, the statement by Cardinal Koenig. The Archbishop of Vienna endorsed the common Bible idea and spoke approvingly of a project concerning a Gospel translation that he knew about behind the Iron Curtain, in Poland. After his statement, Cardinal Koenig remarked, in his modest way, that what Cardinal Alfrink would have to say on the subject would be more important. I asked one other cardinal for an endorsement of the common Bible idea, Cardinal Suenens, the Primate of Belgium. He replied that he had no difficulties about the matter, but that I should consult Cardinal Alfrink, to whom he would defer on a topic involving such specialized knowledge of Scripture.

Cardinal Cushing and Cardinal Suenens both felt, obviously, that an expert in the biblical languages—like Cardinal Alfrink or Cardinal Koenig—was in a better position to talk about biblical questions than they were. I encountered this deference to expert knowledge all along the line. I asked several cardinals about what action the Council might take on social questions; they referred me to Cardinal Suenens, for he was the sociologist among them. To others were left other questions. In every case, the reader may be interested in knowing, I found that Pope John XXIII was regarded as the expert on the Council as a whole. If I asked who emerged as the greatest of the Council Fathers, I got the answer: Pope John XXIII. Cardinal Léger expresses it best of all in the second part of his interview.

One day I asked a Council *peritus,* or expert, who he thought was the most influential of the Council Fathers. He replied: "The little man who wasn't there—Pope John XXIII." One of the things this book proves, however, is that Pope John really was there—everywhere.

I

THE BISHOP

AND THE LAITY

Paul-Emile Cardinal Léger, Archbishop of Montreal, has produced a series of pastoral letters, sermons and addresses that mark him as a leading spokesman of the Church in North America. I interviewed him in Montreal to find out more about some of his key thoughts. The day before I came to his house, the cardinal had consecrated a bishop, Most Reverend Gerald Emmett Carter, D.D., who had invited me to assist at the ceremonies. The cardinal's thoughts, when I interviewed him, were focused (like my own as a result of the consecration ceremony) on the roles of bishop and laity in the life of the Church. The cardinal had been thinking a great deal about the problem of unity, not only among the churches that bear the name Christian, but among the members of the Catholic Church itself. He spoke profoundly and frankly. It was clear that he was much concerned about the image the Church presents to the world.

Cardinal Léger bears striking resemblance to Maurice Richard, the famous Canadian hockey player, but my hour-long conversation in the room whose door bears the inscription *Son Eminence* had nothing to do with sports. With the Second Vatican Council approaching, there were many serious questions to consider in order that the Church might better succeed with her mission in the modern world. The cardinal had many striking ideas and proposals, and he had considerable experience to back them up.

Cardinal Léger was born in Valleyfield, in the Province of Quebec, on April 26, 1904. At the age of twelve he entered the preparatory seminary of Ste Thérèse at Ste Thérèse, Quebec, and completed his classical studies there. He was ordained to the priesthood on May 25, 1929, after studies in theology at the Grand Seminary in Montreal. The following year he entered the Society of St. Sulpice. He went to France and made further studies at the Institut Catholique in Paris. From 1931 to 1933 he taught at the Sulpician seminary at Issy-les-Moulineaux, near Paris. The next six years he spent in Japan, where he established a seminary at Fukuoka. In 1939 he returned to Canada to teach at the Seminary of Philosophy, Montreal, but the next year he was appointed vicar general of his home diocese, Valleyfield, and rector of the cathedral. In 1947 he was sent to Rome as rector of the Pontifical Canadian College. Pope Pius XII named him a domestic prelate.

On March 25, 1950, Monsignor Léger was named Archbishop of Montreal. He was consecrated in Rome on April 26. Less than three years later, in the consistory of January 12, 1953, Pope Pius XII proclaimed the archbishop a cardinal. He was the sixth cardinal in the history of the Canadian hierarchy.

Before I went to see the cardinal, I stepped into the Montreal cathedral, the Basilica of Our Lady Queen of the World. I noticed that the cardinal's *prie-dieu* in the sanctuary was facing the nave and that there was a microphone attached to it. I remembered then that Cardinal Léger was often called the Cardinal of the Rosary, because, ever since 1949, he had been leading a daily broadcast of the rosary over a Montreal station. This was one of his ways of encouraging family prayer. He has led the rosary every night he has been in Montreal.

Cardinal Léger's appointment to the Central Preparatory Commission of the Second Vatican Council meant that there would be many periods when he would be away from Montreal. The significance of these commission meetings for the development of his thoughts came out in the interview. I knew that he had been called the Cardinal of the Poor for some time, and that he had been outspoken on the need for removing slum areas, building low-cost housing, uniting efforts of management and labor to fight the problem of unemployment and a number of other social problems. He had been looking beyond the horizons of the Province of Quebec, to take a wider view of these problems, but, as he admits himself, the meetings with bishops from all over the world have given him an even more international outlook.

QUESTION

Shortly before the World Council of Churches meeting at New Delhi (November 18–December 6, 1961), Your Eminence asked all the Catholics of the Montreal Archdiocese to pray for the success of the meeting. The message must have made a profound impression upon Montreal and the Province of Quebec.

CARDINAL LÉGER

I hope so. It was a call for a basic act of charity, of course, but by it I meant also to give leadership to my people in this matter of Church unity. Concern for unity seems to have become the chief mark of Christianity in our times. It must be due to the inspiration of the Holy Spirit. Under the circumstances, therefore, I regarded it as an exercise of my pastoral office to lead my people in prayer that an important meeting of our separated brethren like that one of the World Council should follow the guidance of the Holy Spirit.

I have watched the ecumenical movement develop in my archdiocese, and I must say I am pleased with the increase of sympathy between leaders of the various Christian groups. I am delighted that Catholic priests and Protestant clergymen meet more often now to engage in fraternal dialogue. There must be such contacts if we are going to do anything about reunion of the members of Christ's Body. I am happy to say that newspapers, radio and television give good coverage to discussions about Church unity in this part of the world.

It was not a new thing that we should ask the Holy Spirit to guide a Protestant group in its deliberations. In the annual Church Unity Octave, that is surely one of the things we pray for. We cannot be indifferent about it. We must do everything in our power to remove the evil of disunity.

Also, it seemed to me then and still does, there is urgency in the fact that Christian disunity results in the pagan world not believing, not heeding, the message and claims of the Church. Pagans look on the Catholic Church as just one of the many Christian denominations. I have thought more and more about this as a result of my frequent meetings with cardinals and bishops from countries around the world who tell me about the image of the Church in their lands. As a member of the Central Preparatory Commission of the Second Vatican Council I spend ten days every month working in Rome, and it is an experience to have one's horizons expanded by these contacts. I had all this in mind when I asked my people to pray that the World Council meeting serve the cause of unity desired by our Lord.

QUESTION

Your Eminence has also entrusted to the people a number of responsibilities. You have said, haven't you, that all laymen without exception must become prophets of the Gospel in their own circles?

CARDINAL LÉGER

Yes. It is not only the Pope and the bishops who are prophets, or witnesses, of the Gospel. The laity are the Church, too, as Pope Pius XII said, because they participate in Christ's offices of king, priest and prophet (that is, teacher) by their baptism. That is something Pope John had in mind when he said, in the encyclical *Ad Petri Cathedram* (June 29, 1959), that the return of separated Christians to unity is linked to the internal renewal of the Catholic Church. The Pope has described that renewal as "a development of Catholic faith, a moral renewal of the Christian life of the faithful, an adaptation of ecclesiastical discipline to the needs and methods of our time." The Pope said then that he expected the Second Vatican Council to be a "wonderful" manifestation of truth, unity and charity, and he hoped that manifestation would appeal to our separated brethren as a "gentle invitation" to seek and find the unity for which our Lord prayed.

In that spirit, I have told the people they must center their lives on the essential realities of the faith and not on peripheral devotions. I have explained that this means going to the Gospel and making it the inspiration of our whole lives. Then we will be prophets, that is, speakers for God or preachers in front of the world. Then we will give our fellowmen a witness of the divine truth. Then we will show them that the Christian life is, above all, a way of life, a living contact with our Lord.

Also, in this way our own people will rediscover many valuable things that were left in the background because Catholic theological thinking had so often concentrated too exclusively on disputed points. A more balanced presentation of the faith should come out of this approach. Again, that is something Pope John has stressed. He hopes that our separated brethren will be drawn to us when we show them this balanced presentation of the faith I have mentioned.

In giving responsibilities to the laity I have also been working to preserve and strengthen unity within the Church itself.

We used to have three priests among the seven members of the Montreal Catholic School Board; now the board is composed entirely of lay people. A layman is now vice rector of our Catholic University of Montreal. I have turned St. Paul's College entirely over to laymen. St. Paul's College is a classical college which was founded and previously directed and staffed by secular priests.

Many of the clergy find it difficult to accept these changes.

It is understandable. It has been a long tradition that priests and religious congregations are the ones who run our seventy-five classical colleges. But I have told my priests that the aspiration of the laity to share in direction of the schools is legitimate, and that we have to take another look at our management of things. I have been encouraging dialogue not only between Catholics and separated Christians but also between Catholic clergy and laity. They must work out some kind of healthy collaboration that respects their roles in the Church.

We have to face the fact that we don't have enough priests and religious to run the schools. It isn't a new fact. One of our schools has had 70 percent of its teaching hours handled by the laity. What I think I do have to stress is that Catholic laymen are true members of the Church and they can give a truly Catholic education, therefore, even when they do not have any priests, brothers or sisters working with them in classrooms or other places where the Church has need of them.

The clergy have to make an act of confidence in the lay members of the Church and show themselves willing to adapt to the demands of the common good. The laity must dedicate themselves completely to concern for the spiritual requirements they are called to take care of, in education and in whatever else the bishop asks of them. The way to look at it is to see that circumstances force some change, but that we are not without a solution, because we have the laity, who are true witnesses of the Gospel and can be called to come in and take over where they are needed. It takes some courage, on both sides, to see it this way, but our Lord has not left us without the grace to do it.

Our Lord gave us the Holy Spirit to unite us in the perfect bond of peace, but that, of course, presupposes hearts dilated by the action of charity. It has come home to me again and again that the Holy Spirit is given to a bishop in order that he may be His instrument in the building up of the Mystical Body of Christ. In a very true sense, it is because of the bishop that the Church here or there is one. The bishop must be the guardian of unity, with love for all and with respect for the gifts God has given to each. It is not easy, but with the help of the Holy Spirit it can be done.

Among our professional and intellectual people there are severe critics of the bishop and the clergy. Yes, we have anticlericalism, especially on the part of those severe critics who rail against what they call "conformism." I call upon our laity for a solution to this problem. If we have enough profoundly Christian laymen who are aware of their responsibilities, we shall convince the people that they are the Church and they have a vital role to play.

QUESTION

You have given some striking directives, Your Eminence, to guide priests and people who are engaged in the teaching of religion. You have shown that their work constitutes a combined biblical, liturgical and catechetical apostolate. Would you say something about the biblical approach in the Province of Quebec and about your Bible Center in Montreal?

CARDINAL LÉGER

On a number of occasions I have questioned whether our religious education has been too abstract and dry. I have approved the movement toward getting back to the message of salvation and focusing attention on the person of Christ that we find in the Gospels. Instead of stress on individual piety and on "moral preoccupations," I have advocated greater awareness of active participation in the life of the Church as we find it proposed in St. Paul's Epistles. In the official program of religion for the elementary schools of the Province of Quebec there is a carefully worked-out concordance between the New Testament and the various grades in the religion course. In their seventh year at school, the pupils see the whole New Testament picture chronologically.

The teachers of religion hand on not merely doctrines but a

living faith in the Christ of revelation. The pupils should derive from the course a notion of the Kingdom of God and God's plan of salvation revealed in His Son, who acts in His Church through the Holy Spirit. The education they get stresses their response to the message of the living God, throughout all of the life that God has given them, including the social, cultural, economic and political aspects of it.

The Bible Center you refer to works closely with the Catechetical Center that directs the religious programs of the archdiocese. Incidentally, the two centers are in the same building, and the combined operation is an interesting example of cooperation between clergy and laity. The directors are priests; administration has been entrusted to Knights of the Holy Sepulchre; members of a secular institute staff the offices; groups of teachers—religious and laity—come in for briefing sessions.

The Bible Center puts out a weekly folder that is made available in quantity to parish churches throughout the archdiocese. The front page of the leaflet shows a striking photograph or design that illustrates a place or theme connected with the essay on biblical theology and verses for daily meditation that are given inside. On the back page, questions people have sent in are answered by one of our biblical scholars. Father Jean Martucci, director of the Bible Center, gives weekly conferences in the Hotel Dieu auditorium for four hundred, sometimes six hundred, people, and he appears on TV every Sunday afternoon for half an hour at five o'clock. All this helps the people to understand the liturgy, which is made up so largely of passages from the Bible.

QUESTION

In 1960, Your Eminence brought out a pastoral directory on the Mass. This directory gave detailed rules about participation in the Mass according to the decrees of the Holy See. Are you pleased with the response of your people?

CARDINAL LÉGER

I now have parishes where a thousand people sing the Mass like angels. And the directory, I am pleased to say, has carried its influence beyond the archdiocese—to Europe, as well. That book and the booklet that the people use in accordance with it (*Livret des Fidèles*) took a lot of work to produce, but they would be dead letters unless priests and people cooperated in putting them into effect. I might mention also that the English translation of the pastoral directory is ready for the printer and should be out in a few weeks.

I put priests and people under strict obligation to follow the prescriptions of the directory. The clergy who responded immediately have produced remarkable results. Seminarians and religious in training now get a liturgical and pastoral formation that harmonizes with the directory. In some parishes, of course, the pace has been slower. Pastoral prudence has demanded a more gradual application of the directory in those places. But I have told the people that if they think their clergy haven't done anything, or haven't done enough, they should go to them and offer their services to get things done. And I have urged them to assist the clergy who have things going well by searching out the people who don't yet see the need for active participation in the liturgy and helping them to see the light.

QUESTION

I noticed that Montreal's large daily paper La Presse *gave front-page headlines to your commentary on Pope John's encyclical "Christianity and Social Progress" (Mater et Magistra).* La Presse *ran your text in installments for three days in a row. This was leadership in social thinking, recognized as such by the daily press. Quite an achievement, wasn't it?*

CARDINAL LÉGER

Well, it was an occasion for leadership, certainly, when that encyclical came out and discussions arose. The idea of socialization, as understood by the Pope, was to be applied to our area, I felt, and someone had to explain just how. Also, I wanted to stress that the encyclical called the laity to action. It is the special task of the laity to bring the social teaching of the Church to fulfillment. Unless they do something about it, that very teaching is actually incomplete.

When I was invited to address the Chamber of Commerce, I felt here was a good occasion to make sure that people understand the difference between socialization and socialism, and also to say a number of other things I felt needed saying. It may have seemed harsh when I said that we Canadians are overfed people, egotistic and indifferent, no longer seeing beyond our "wheat curtain." But I am so appalled when I realize that 60 percent of the world's people go hungry or do not have what is necessary. One comes to see that it is scandalous to live as we do when there are hungry, dying people in underdeveloped countries. It is not right that we should consider such a situation as normal.

I feel strongly that if Canada only had a rational immigration policy, our country could welcome hundreds of thousands of immigrants, and our standard of living would not go down. Instead, Canadians go on thinking that hunger in the world is only a legend told by missionaries and world travelers. When I think that a Canadian's life expectancy is sixty-five years and that of a man in India is only thirty, I ask myself how we can sleep without worrying. We need lay people with good instruction in the social teaching of the Church who will see to it that public opinion is educated to the needs of other peoples and that government provides emergency help and technical assistance and welcomes immigrants. We need men who will see to it that Canada's contribution is not the modest—or rather, insufficient—thing it now is.

QUESTION

You are very frank. It takes courage to speak out like that. You will have opposition, but you are right in giving leader-

*ship and in attempting to create a climate of charity and
apostolic concern. It is not an easy task, is it?*

CARDINAL LÉGER

The task, the mission, of a bishop is not an easy one, especially
in a society that is being molded and formed by scientific
and technological advances and the demands that accompany
them. If the bishop speaks out as a father, there are those who
will give him a hard time on the grounds that he is indulging
in unacceptable paternalism. If the bishop comes out with
directives, he meets with resistance from those who charge he
has infringed upon one or another of their freedoms. If he
doesn't come out with something, he is charged with curry-
ing the favor of the rich. If he backs those who are doing
something for the common good, he is accused of interfering
in temporal matters. He might think he is acting in the best
interests of the country, but some will call him a reactionary
or a carry-over from an obsolete and decadent civilization.

There is a lot of talk these days, in my country as well as
yours, about the pluralistic society in which we live. Now,
conditions vary from place to place, but, whatever the restive
critics I've just been mentioning may think or say, we can
assert it as a fact that we abandon nothing of the faith if we
admit we must make some adaptations. There is no point in
trying to be a medieval man today.

I agree with Cardinal Lercaro, Archbishop of Bologna,
that our respect for the liberty of others is not a concession
suggested by prudence but a new development of principles
that are permanent in our religion. I have looked into this
somewhat, back as far as the writings of the Fathers. Faith,
it is their constant teaching, is a gift, and it is no good trying
to force it on others. I think, for example, of that sentence
in a letter of St. Gregory the Great where he says those who
try to force people into the Church work out their own will
rather than the will of God.

Pope Pius XII made it clear to me that we follow a good
tradition in this country when we respect the conscience and

the rights of non-Catholics, and that we are in line with the thinking of the Church. In an address to Italian lawyers in 1953, the Pope stated it is not an absolute principle that doctrinal and moral deviation should be suppressed wherever possible on the grounds that tolerating it is in itself immoral. God, he added, has never given such an absolute principle, and he recalled the parable of the weeds, in which Christ said the weeds should be left to grow up with the wheat. On higher principles, therefore, it is permissible, and sometimes it is better, not to suppress error. One can take this position for a greater good. That speech of Pope Pius XII is something to read and read again, especially for those who live, or try to live, the Christian life in our big, complicated urban centers, like Montreal.

Perhaps no one worked harder than Cardinal Léger during the preparations for the Council. No Council Father followed everything more closely than Cardinal Léger when the sessions actually began. He spoke often during the Council, and everyone recognized him as a leader. When I visited him again at his residence in Montreal, toward the end of March, 1963, he was much thinner than when I had seen him a year earlier. The years of Council work, I knew, had so tired him that in January he spent a week in a hospital recovering from heart fatigue, but a reply from him during that period had reassured me that he was all right, and I was pleased to discover, when I came to his room, that he was certainly his old self. There was a significant difference, however. He was still lively and forceful when he spoke; he warmed to his theme; but he was more serene now. He had worried much, and suffered much, for his sensitive nature had felt keenly the burden of delays, difficulties and frustrations in the preparatory work of the Council, but now he was confident and optimistic. The day I visited him, radio and TV news bulletins announced that Cardinal Léger was a member of the new Commission on Canon Law that the Pope had formed to work out legislative details after the Council's conclusion. The work of the Council would go on, therefore, although nobody knew how long it would take. The prospect of the continued work did not dismay Cardinal Léger at all. I soon learned why he was so serene and confident.

QUESTION

You were one of the most faithful Fathers of the Council, Your Eminence. You missed none of the sessions of the Central Preparatory Commission, and, as far as I know, you missed none of the sessions of the Council itself and of the commissions to which you belonged. How does it all look to you now?

CARDINAL LÉGER

I did work very hard, and for a long time it was a matter of having faith in the Council. But now I do not have *faith* in the Council. Faith is the substance of things unseen. Now I *see* the great reality of the Council that has emerged from our work. I have no need of faith in a fruitful outcome of the Council's work, because now I *see* the great fruit of the Council. Along the way I gave a good bit of myself to the cause. I have lost forty pounds since the work of the Council began.

QUESTION

On my recent visits to European Council Fathers, they have told me that the trend which developed at the Council is irreversible. Is it this trend you refer to when you speak of the great fruit of the Council?

CARDINAL LÉGER

Let me put it this way. In discourses before the Council and on the opening day of the Council, Pope John expressed his ardent hope and desire that the Council would succeed in presenting to the world the splendid visage of the Church which she had when she came forth into the world. I believe this has been done. For me, therefore, the Council is a great

success. You see, this is what has happened. All the bishops
of the Church assembled with their head, Peter's successor,
the Vicar of Christ. Thus assembled, they asked: Who are
we? More accurately still, the Church thus assembled asked:
Who am I?

In answering the parts to this question, we were ascending a
great staircase. Above us the Pope beckoned, and we labored
to reach him. The going was hard sometimes, but we would
finally arrive where he stood. Then he would point up, ahead,
and we would see that the staircase went on higher in such a
direction that earlier we would not have seen this continuation. And there he would be again, beckoning us.

From the very beginning, all of us had the awareness that
we were meeting with the Holy Father, and we desired that it
should be a true meeting of minds. We would have a variety
of ideas, a variety of opinions about how and where to place
stresses in our teaching, but we certainly all intended to
arrive where the Holy Father would stand, and to be with
him. I often have thought how, standing there with his hands
folded, he looked like a man holding out a beautiful flower, a
luminous thing, in his strong hands. Pope John himself said,
you remember: "We have felt that it was God's lofty command that caused the thought of celebrating an Ecumenical
Council to rise like the flower of an early and unexpected
springtime within us soon after our elevation to the pontifical
throne." As we made our way up the great staircase toward
him, it seemed to me that, by raising his hands, he sent forth
light from the flower so that the steps ahead were illuminated.
And the flower itself seemed to blossom more brilliantly. At a
certain point in our ascent it seemed that the answer to the
question "Who am I?" was being given so that we, Holy
Father and bishops and all in union with us, were seen as the
Church, in such a way that it was like the heavenly Jerusalem
descending—the Church, with the wrinkles of distortion and
the mistakes of time (the result of human errors, emotions
and feelings) removed.

Now, this effort of the Church to present herself to the world with her original splendor and beauty has already succeeded in drawing the world to her. I can assure you, I have seen it happening in a number of areas. It is the work of the Holy Spirit that we have succeeded in making this presentation to the world. It is a gift of Divine Providence that Pope John is the man he is. Now, when he speaks, the world listens more attentively. He speaks, and the whole Council speaks with him. The Church manifests herself to the world, and she is given the attention that she and her message deserve. It will be clearly seen someday how much the Pope and the Council have affected the current of events, drawing souls, saving them from darkness and bringing them to light.

When we assemble again, to continue the sessions of the Council, I am sure that we can finish up very soon, because the vision of the Church we have now is so compelling, so attractive that we can communicate it through the decrees of the Council. If we do nothing else than finish the *schema* on the Church, we will have done enough, and I think we have already achieved it. We can leave the details to commissions that will continue their work after the closing of the Council, such as the Commission on Canon Law which has been announced. I am quite confident that the vision of the Church I have described to you will continue to inspire the work of the commissions. It will continue to inspire the bishops when they return to their sees. Periodically, a certain number of them will journey to Rome for the meetings of their commissions (the rapidity of modern transportation and communication is providential in this matter) and thus on into the future we will have a continuation of the Council functioning along with the Roman Curia. The Curia, as the executive arm of the Holy Father, and the commissions, as the voice of the bishops working on a particular task, will function together as the Holy Father and the bishops function together in the Council.

QUESTION

Your Eminence's optimism and confidence are in striking contrast to reports of critical comments that you were said to have made shortly after your return from the first session of the Council.

CARDINAL LÉGER

I was disappointed—in fact, I was hurt—that certain remarks I made about the preparatory work of the Council were taken as criticism of the Council itself. I explained this to my people in my annual New Year's message. As I said then, I have too great an admiration for the sincerity and seriousness of the Council deliberations to judge the work of the Council Fathers unfavorably. What was the first thing I said about the Council when I returned to Montreal? I told reporters at the airport: "I cannot express all the feelings in my heart and soul. The Council was both a human and divine experience." I stressed then how the presence of Protestant and Orthodox observers at the Council made this Council unique in the history of the Church, that their presence and our work showed the Church has an open mind and is unafraid to work with witnesses from the world looking on. "The reaction of the world has been good," I stressed. I said: "It is impossible to explain all of its worth." I said: "I think we have communicated . . . I think we have left something to follow." From all reports, I told them, it is evident that the Council was a great event. We cannot close our eyes to it. I have seen the evidence of the Council's influence mounting ever since, and I can say what I said then with much more force.

A few days later, I spoke to an audience made up of members of Catholic Action groups of Montreal. When I described for them what the first session of the Council was like, I went back to the beginning and recalled what the *schemata* were like when they were presented to the Council. As everybody knows now, much of what was in the *schemata* proposed for the consideration of the Fathers of the Council was juridical and academic in tone. When we had it in front of us at the Council, we could see that the *schemata* were not pastoral enough; there was not enough of the *aggiornamento* that Pope John had called for. Now, by nature I am impulsive. My people know me; they know I want to get things going and get things done. As I recalled those *schemata* and how they looked when we were all assembled and considering them, I told my people we realized what had been done would have to be done over. In fact, talking to my people that night, I treated this with humor; I did not scowl and scold. I had said earlier, remember, that the Council was both a human and a divine experience. Now, the work of preparation for the Council was valuable and important, but it was only an introductory phase of the Council's work. It did not enjoy the same charismatic guidance as the work of the Council itself assembled in session. So one could make judgments about the preparatory phase that need not be applied to the Council itself, which is guided by the Holy Spirit in a special way. I am not the only one who criticized the preparatory work. It is no secret that the votes of the bishops amounted to such a criticism. So, then, we had to do it over; we had to have a coordinating commission that would provide directives; we had to have simplified *schemata*; we had to get down to the essentials in a language appropriate to (and understandable to) the people we were trying to reach.

I can tell you that I am quite happy with the progress that has been made between the sessions of the Council, by the Coordinating Commission and the other commissions working with its directives. They have worked in the light of the vision of the Church that I have described to you. They have worked to keep the Church young, by redefining the functions of bishops, clergy and laity. The care of souls—and the renewal and rejuvenation of the Church that is required for this—has been their guiding norm. They have asked: Who am I? And they have asked: What is my mission? In other words, they have been carrying forward the examination of conscience that the Council is making for the Church, to see if it is responding to the Church's mission as Christ our Lord conceived it. They have been practical. They pared the *schemata* down to manageable size. In the process, they have cut out repetitions and too-detailed discussions (which they have assigned to postconciliar commissions).

QUESTION

How long do you think it will take for the Council and the postconciliar commissions to finish the work of the Second Vatican Council?

CARDINAL LÉGER

Now that we have succeeded in grasping the idea Pope John had about the Council, we can finish the formal sessions of the Council well before Christmas of 1963, I think. The length of the work of the commissions will vary—perhaps five, ten, fifteen or twenty years, depending on the complexity of the details they will have to deal with. Implementation of the Council's decisions, and the commissions' decrees—who knows how long that will take? Remember, after the Council of Trent legislated on seminaries, it took a long time for the achievement to materialize. With regard to the laity, for example, I have sometimes thought that bringing them into the greater participation in the Mass that will come after the Council could take ten years. Taking into account all the functions of the laity that the Council can or will determine, I sometimes think perhaps one should say that within a century the Church will be young and modern. There, you see how much more patient I have become!

QUESTION

Like the Holy Father himself, you now take a long-range view of the Council's work.

CARDINAL LÉGER

Let me conclude with a word about Pope John. I have great affection for the person of the Holy Father, as I have told my people on several occasions. My people know—I have told them —that one of my most cherished duties as their bishop is to develop in my people the same love and affection for the Holy Father that I have. There are many reasons for my attachment to Pope John. During the years of his pontificate, I have learned from him the virtues which are characteristic of true shepherds. Thanks to him, I have been able to remain in peace and serenity in the difficulties which every bishop meets, for I have always found in him an understanding father. When I returned to Montreal from the first session of the Council, my people asked me about the Holy Father's health. Their question and my answer were inspired by genuine concern and filial respect for the Holy Father. Here, again, erroneous impressions were conveyed in reports of my answer, but when I visited Pope John subsequently, I found him, as always, a remarkable treasure-house of patience and kindness and understanding.

Again, the main thing to remember is that the Holy Spirit is working through Pope John. Through him, and through all of us in union with him, the Spirit of Christ is working. The Spirit is moving us more and more profoundly in the quest for unity. The desire for the unity of all Christians was a great part of what animated Pope John to call this Council. As we prayed and studied together at the Council, we bishops felt this desire spreading throughout the Church. We knew we had to find the best means of presenting the Gospel of Jesus Christ to the twentieth-century world; and everything at the Council—the interventions of the Council Fathers, the work of the theologians and the commissions, the presence and observations of the non-Catholic delegate-observers— everything reminded us that we had to do something to break down the barriers that separate the various Christian confessions. The presence of the delegate-observers—our Christian brothers who do not share our faith fully but who are also animated by this great desire—was an inspiration for us. Their presence reminded us constantly that eventually the Council should give its position on important questions concerning unity: the question of what the Church is and what her proper unity is; the general pastoral directives for the Church's ecumenical work; the question of religious liberty. The presence of the observers reminded us constantly of Pope John's clear statement in the address on the opening day that "the substance of the ancient teaching of the deposit of faith is one thing, the manner in which it is expressed is another. It is therefore not only possible but necessary to clothe this teaching in forms which are accessible and attractive to the way men think today." The presence of the observers reminded us to think this way about the Church's teaching about herself, her authority, the apostolic succession, the Holy Father's office as Peter's successor and the teaching mission of the Church. Their presence reminded us to be sure we rid ourselves of historical and psychological prejudices and that we manifest love for our separated brethren as brothers in Christ.

The whole experience of the Second Vatican Council adds up to a source of great hopes for the bishops. We join with Pope John in expressing the wish that these hopes will be realized in full. Our wish is confronted by the realities of world problems, but, as I say, I have already seen world problems influenced by appreciation of the renewed visage of the Church, and I have expectations that the peace we seek in our times will come nearer—has come nearer—because of the Council. If great differences in social conditions are not a favorable climate for peace, we shall find those differences crumbling before the light and grace streaming from the renewed Church. If the foundations of society are weakened by wounds inflicted upon family life by divorce, we shall nevertheless see more and more people drawn to the light and grace of the Church. If peace in the world is withheld from us by the plight of the hungry, the lepers, the deaf, the blind, the mentally retarded, the aged, the refugees and others who cannot compete in a demanding world, we shall nevertheless see what the light of Christ, light of the nations, can do to stimulate those who should help such unfortunate ones and thus contribute to peace in our times.

II

THE COUNCIL,

PRIESTS AND THE LAITY

One day in October, 1948, a white-haired don, the Reverend
Leslie Walker, S.J., led a group of properly gowned new students
through the streets of Oxford to the great room where the vice
chancellor of the university sat. With me in that group from
Campion Hall walked a young priest from the new nation of
Pakistan. Standing together before the vice-chancellor, we were
solemnly proclaimed members of the University. *"Ego vos mem-
bra hujus Universitatis facio,"* said the vice-chancellor, speaking
the language of Duns Scotus at the very place where the thir-
teenth-century theologian had delivered his lectures in Latin.
The Pakistani priest, Father Joseph Cordeiro, spent three years
at Oxford studying "P.P.E." or "Modern Greats"—philosophy,
politics and economics. A few years after he took his degree,
Father Cordeiro was rector of a seminary in Pakistan. In 1958,
he became Archbishop of Karachi, Pakistan's largest city.

At the time of his appointment, Archbishop Cordeiro was
only thirty-nine years old—the youngest archbishop in the
world. He was the first Pakistani to become a bishop, and he was
named directly to the first position in the hierarchy. Less than
four years later, he was on his way to the Second Vatican Council.

The archbishop visited me in New York, and we made a trip
through New England to call upon three university professors
who had been students with us at Oxford. The archbishop

stopped at several places to visit parents of Franciscan Missionaries of Mary, Medical Mission Sisters, Daughters of the Heart of
Mary and Dominican cloistered nuns now working in Pakistan.

As we rode along, we talked about the archbishop's hopes and
expectations concerning the coming Council. He was certain
that the concept of a bishop as a "successor of the Apostles"
would be stressed early in the Council. It had been one of the
main items left over from the First Vatican Council. Incidentally, the archbishop commented that the Council would no
doubt decree that a bishop may hear confessions anywhere in
the world. "As it is now," he said, "I can delegate faculties to
any priest I meet to hear my confession, but ordinarily I cannot
hear his confession." According to present Church law, only
cardinals may hear confessions anywhere in the world. All other
priests must request "faculties" or permission to hear confessions
from the bishop of the diocese where they wish to hear the
confessions.

Archbishop Cordeiro does not wear the touch of red below his
collar that Americans have come to associate with bishops and
monsignors. The ring on his finger is the only external sign of
his high rank. I discovered that, though he was deeply conscious
of being a successor to the apostles, he did not set much store by
external signs of the episcopal dignity today. His priests and
people know him and respect him for his apostolic office; he is
content to let others judge him on the facts of his leadership.

I wondered if the archbishop's views on dispensing with the
externals of ecclesiastical rank might not be partly the result
of living in a country that was less than 0.5-percent Catholic
(in fact, 95.5-percent Muslim and 4-percent Hindu). I had
heard that he drove around his archdiocese in a little Fiat, and
I wondered if that might not be due to the fact that in his country only the wealthy can afford to own a car. But as he talked
about the office and duties of a bishop, I realized that he had
taken quite literally the stress upon humility and patience in
the ceremonies of a bishop's consecration. He wanted to mingle

with the people the way Peter and Paul had, the way Christ Himself had.

We talked about the spread of the Church in the time of the Apostles, about the way they had preached the faith, and about Pope John's statement that he had convoked the Council in order to secure a presentation of the faith in all its "primitive splendor." For twelve consecutive weeks, Archbishop Cordeiro had filled half a page in each issue of his archdiocesan newspaper explaining what the coming Council was and what it could do. Here and there in the world press, he had noticed, statements crop up that previous Councils dealt with crises (heresy or schism, for example) but the Second Vatican Council was not occasioned by a crisis. It *was* occasioned by a crisis, the archbishop insisted. As he saw it, it was not so much a crisis of Communism or the spread of materialism and secularism, though these were real threats to right order. It was, rather, a crisis of scientism (something quite different from science, of course) or technologism. To meet the mind of man that was being molded by these phenomena, the Church had to act. The message of salvation was in danger of becoming unintelligible to great masses of modern man. Lest the faith be thought irrelevant by the new masses, there had to be a reexamination of our presentation of it. There had to be, in fact, a re-presentation of the faith in the language of our times.

A bishop's primary function is to teach, the archbishop stressed; and in that teaching he must be faithful to the deposit of faith handed down by the Apostles. He added that the biblical and liturgical movements, and the trend in teaching religion that would stress the essentials of the faith in biblical terms, were providential helps for reaching the people with the Good News of salvation. One could not just go on teaching the faith the way one learned it in seminary days, he emphasized. The language of the people around us changes. We must talk to them about the faith in their language. So often, he said, it turns out that a return to the biblical imagery reaches the minds and hearts of the people, whereas early twentieth-century and nine-teenth-century abstract and philosophical terminology in the teaching of religion does not.

His priests are a bishop's chief help in the teaching and preaching of the faith, the archbishop said, but unfortunately, the idea that a priest should keep up his studies has come to be regarded by all too many as almost impossible. Many, in fact, regard it as simply incompatible with their job. But how can they do their job properly, he asked, if they do not keep reading and studying? Today, in Europe and the United States, as well as in Asia, the archbishop often meets people who are disturbed by newspaper reports about new interpretations of Scripture. It certainly does not help, he observed, when pastors and priests simply manifest the same distress. They should know what the biblical scholars are doing, and they should explain it to the people, in order to close the gap between biblical research and the ordinary layman's knowledge of the Bible. Then the people would understand that, in some cases, thanks to the labors of experts in ancient languages and ancient history, we have rediscovered the authentic, original understanding of certain passages in the Bible. Now we see more clearly, for example, that when Jesus said "Make friends of the mammon of iniquity," He was speaking ironically, not literally. We no longer have to labor to explain that passage seriously, the way even some Fathers of the Church did. How easy it is, said the archbishop, for a priest to explain such things, briefly and to the point, if he has kept up with developments.

So many priests go back to their books, however, only when they are forced to do so by some problem they have run into. Was it during their seminary years that the desire to keep studying withered, the archbishop wondered? If so, he said, something in that seminary training had to be changed. One does not need a survey, he observed, to be convinced that a very small percentage of priests keep up with their studies in the true sense of the word, and this percentage might be lower in mission countries. He suspected the difficulty was that seminary studies were not sufficiently presented in a way that enabled the student to see they would be useful to him in his future pastoral duties. That seemed to be why there was now a separation between pastoral ministry and study in the minds of so many priests. He agreed with Archbishop Denis Hurley, of Durban, South Africa, who wrote in the Irish *Furrow* (January, 1962) that the principal preoccupation of the seminary should be to mold its pupils into competent "communicators of faith." As Archbishop Hurley said, the chief object of the seminary is not to impart academic knowledge but to impart communicable knowledge. What good does it do, Archbishop Cordeiro asked, if at the end of his seminary duties a young priest has a good knowledge of the faith in terms of magisterial decrees and scholastic definitions? As Archbishop Hurley put it: "The big question is, has he a communicable knowledge? . . . Ask the parishioners in the pews. Ask the teachers in the schools. It would be a miracle if the answer were in the affirmative."

Archbishop Cordeiro practices what he preaches. I discovered that, besides reading *America* each week, he has for some years been following *Worship, Theology Digest, Theological Studies,* the *Catholic Biblical Quarterly,* and several British and European theological publications. He obviously knew and understood what modern biblical and theological experts were talking about. He told me the priest cannot be outdone by others in an age when success depends so much on professional knowledge. The progress of biblical studies and of theology simply demands continuous study and reflection, if the priest is going to make relevant applications to the needs of the times. If the priest does not teach, explain and defend the faith to the satisfaction of his hearers, especially sophisticated modern, educated audiences, the public estimation of the Church will suffer.

There is serious danger in only half-digested ideas of theology, the archbishop said. It could be seen in the consequences of false direction, he added, or in the improper use of scriptural texts. He recalled the warning of St. Francis de Sales to his priests: "I tell you in truth that ignorance in priests is more to be feared than sin. . . ." He recalled, too, a recent series of articles by laymen in a magazine for the clergy. Several of the writers had expressed strong desire for more dogma in sermons, more of the joyous message of Christ to man, that they might have life and have it more abundantly.

Besides being a teacher of the faith, the archbishop pointed out, a priest is also the judge of consciences and the director of souls. In this capacity, he said, the priest could easily be found excusing himself from the need to study, on the grounds that his people are ignorant, or "not that well educated," and that confessions are not a serious affair—"one or two mortal sins; for the rest, confessions of devotion, etc." But, he insisted, in every parish and institution there will be chosen souls, probably more than the priest realizes. To guide those souls up the path of perfection requires skill and training. Unfortunately, we often hear that there is no priest to direct souls because the priest does not have the time or the ability. It was true, the archbishop admitted, that giving individual spiritual direction was well down the list of a priest's essential duties, after the providing of a proper liturgy and the teaching of the faith, but it was a part of his job, and he could do it only if he kept reading and studying.

It takes time to read and study, of course, and everywhere throughout the Church we have the problem of insufficient priests. I asked the archbishop therefore if he favored the idea of a lay diaconate to help priests in administration of sacraments and in teaching the faith. Archbishop James P. Davis, of San Juan, Puerto Rico, had just said there was likelihood that the ancient office of the lay diaconate might be revived by the Second Vatican Council; under such a revival, he had said, "even married men" could be ordained to the office of deacon after proper preparation. Such an arrangement, Archbishop Davis had said, would greatly aid the work of the Church in mission areas where there are shortages of priests and religious vocations.

Archbishop Cordeiro replied that he was "not too enthusiastic" about the idea. He knew there were many countries where the bishops would not favor the idea of a lay diaconate, because the people would find much difficulty in accepting it. This fact, he thought, would become apparent when all the bishops assembled at the Ecumenical Council. "It will take a long time," he said, "before the people of those lands I refer to will accept lay deacons." He suggested that an experiment along the lines of lay people with minor orders or lay brothers with greater powers would be easier to try out. He was also much interested in the idea of bishops sharing priests in what has been called a "common market" plan. He was keenly interested, for example, in the "Seminary of Europe" at Maastricht, in the Netherlands, that trains seminarians who have volunteered to work in priest-poor parts of Europe. If, he said, there were many immigrants in a diocese that had few priests, but there were more priests in the country from which the people came, why not arrange loans of priests? The work of Cardinal Cushing in founding the Society of St. James the Apostle was an inspiration to the archbishop. According to Cardinal Cushing's plan, priests of the Archdiocese of Boston and other dioceses may volunteer to serve for five years in Latin America without losing their seniority status in the home diocese. The cardinal has loaned priests to many places in North America on similar terms.

A pooling of "priestpower," Archbishop Cordeiro said, would provide continuation of an important approach to pastoral problems that, it seemed to him, foreign-missionary clergy frequently observed better than diocesan clergy of the country itself. Foreigners, brought up in a Catholic environment quite different from that of the mission countries to which they come, are quick to observe differences and to realize the need for adaptation, the need to absorb the good from the native culture. Foreigners are quick to apply themselves, quick to apply the principle of the Church that in every new country the Church should adapt herself to the culture of the place. The diocesan clergy of the place have grown up and lived among the people, and they do not advert so readily to the differences and the problems around them; they are sometimes inclined to excuse themselves on grounds of good faith, without even attempting to study the problems or to find solutions.

The archbishop recalled Pope Pius XII saying, in the encyclical *Evangelii Praecones* (on the missions):

The gospel once preached in any land should not destroy or extinguish whatever the people possess that is naturally good, just and beautiful. For when the Church calls people to a higher culture and a better way of life under the inspiration of the Christian religion, it does not act like one who recklessly fells and uproots a thriving forest. No, she grafts the good stock upon the wild, that it may bear a crop of more delicious fruit.

This means, the archbishop pointed out, that a number of subjects must engage the attention of the priest, e.g., the predominant religious and philosophical systems of the country, the language, local conditions of work and living.

The reference to language brought up the question of the vernacular in the liturgy. Archbishop Cordeiro strongly favored more vernacular in the Mass, for the benefit of the people, since the Mass is the worship of the whole Church—the people, not only the priest. He stressed, however, that it was the first part of the Mass (the Mass of the Catechumens) which needed primary attention. Since that whole first part of the Mass was obviously intended for the instruction of the people, how much better the instruction could be, and how much better their participation in the Mass would be, if the people could hear it in their own tongue. Equally strongly, the archbishop favors keeping Latin as the language of the priest's breviary. It was quite necessary, he held, to keep Latin as the language of the priest's study and prayer. Again, it would take time to get an adequate knowledge of Latin, but the time would have to be found if the priest was to have proper understanding of the Church's documents, the teaching of the Fathers and Doctors of the Church, the liturgical texts and the traditional Latin editions of Bible and breviary.

Once again we had come back to the problem of finding time for the priest to read and study, as well as to do an adequate job of his pastoral work. This time the archbishop suggested that another way of increasing the role of the laity would help.

In so many places, he observed, priests were still doing jobs that the laity could do just as well and probably better. For example, he said, why should priests labor over curriculums in geography, history, mathematics and the sciences for parochial school systems? We have laymen who are experts in all branches of education, the archbishop said. "Let them take over in all these cases," he added. "It is the efficient thing to do," he continued, "and you must remember that the Apostles did try to be efficient in their running of the Church." The archbishop mentioned he had appointed a layman vice principal of the teacher-training college in Karachi, and he had taken steps to set up a lay advisory board for the schools of his archdiocese. He was quite happy that in these actions he was in the company of such a distinguished churchman as Cardinal Léger, of Montreal.

Schools were very much on the archbishop's mind. In his country the Church faces a special problem, because the Catholic schools are much better than many others. High officials of the government have expressed admiration for the schools run by the Church, and, in fact, the archbishop said, Pakistan is one of the countries where religious tolerance is an accepted principle. But Pakistan is 95-percent Muslim, and nationalistic feelings run strong. The archbishop pointed to country after country in Asia and Africa where a similar situation prevails. The bishops of these lands, he said, are convinced that it will not do the Church any good to let Catholic children, the future Church, grow up with a ghetto mentality. These bishops are going to the Council with much to tell their brother bishops of the more developed countries. Archbishop Cordeiro will tell them that his kind of situation underlines the wisdom of stressing student hostels, Newman centers and aggregated colleges at state universities. Besides, he cannot afford to build a whole separate system of parochial schools and Catholic colleges, and he knows that most bishops in Europe and the Americas cannot afford it either. Teamwork, with the state or local community as well as between bishops and priests and the laity, is his solution to most practical problems.

His mention of teamwork at this point reminded the archbishop of the teamwork he had observed among priests in several countries, but most recently in California. In San Jose, he told me, fifteen young priests meet each month, not to complain or to construct castles in the air, but to tell each other what they have done. They compare their actions with theoretical principles; they examine devotions flourishing in their parishes and ask what dogmatic basis they have; they study the principles underlying intellectual, moral and religious problems of their parishioners and discuss how learned and zealous pastors have solved them. This kind of meeting stimulates the priest who might otherwise do little reading and studying; it is an antidote for the priest who might otherwise read only passively; it is conducive to communitarian life among priests.

"Communitarian life?" I said. "Isn't that something for which a man enters a religious order?" "Yes," he replied, "but remember what Pope Pius XII said: 'The Church has already expressed her wish that the practice of the common life should be introduced among the clergy of one parish, or of several neighboring parishes, and this we now strongly recommend and approve.' " In fact, the archbishop added, communitarian life is inherent in the very structure of the Church. Just as the bishop forms one community with his priests and people, so does the parish priest with his assistants. Much has been written in lighter vein about the relations between pastors and assistants, he said. Much of that writing speaks about the distance between the two, but pastor and assistant should be like junior and senior partners in a work of close collaboration. Teamwork in rectories, he added, as well as apostolic efficiency in general, might be helped if the Council legislates a mandatory retirement age for pastors and other Church officials.

Bishops and pastors simply must furnish the means, facilities and incentives for meetings of priests, the archbishop stressed. Those meetings can be very efficient means of increasing communicable knowledge. In an hour, for example, an author can give a group of priests the substance of his book, or the priests can tell one another about their reading and so pool their experience. Pope Pius XII once described religious life today as anemic, because, among learned and manual workers alike, there was ignorance of spiritual matters "which is at times almost complete." This ignorance, the Pope said, must be grappled with and conquered. The Pope added: "Such a task falls primarily on the clergy, and for this reason We implore our Venerable Brethren in the episcopate to leave nothing undone so that priests fully satisfy such a grave obligation (To Italian Men of Catholic Action, September 7, 1947). This, I could see, was uppermost in the archbishop's mind as he made his way to the Council.

I could see, too, that he was still the same priest I had known fifteen years earlier. He had acquired gravity and dignity, but he carried it well. When he spoke, he spoke as one having authority. Yet he was still gentle. As I learned from him what he thought the future of the Church looked like in Asia, I saw that he was patient, strong, courageous. He was going to the Council with many things to offer.

I I I

THE PEOPLE

OF THE CHURCH

Léon-Joseph Cardinal Suenens, Archbishop of Malines-Brussels
and Primate of Belgium, has written books on marriage, the
Church's missionary role, Belgium's controversial school question and Moral Rearmament. In addition to years of study in
religious sociology and a professorship in moral philosophy, after
he had earned doctorates in philosophy and theology and a
degree in Canon Law, he gathered practical experience as chaplain of the Belgian Catholic Film League, chairman of the
Interdiocesan Catholic Press Commission, spiritual adviser of the
Catholic Radio and Television Center and of the Legion of
Mary.

The future cardinal was born on July 16, 1904, at Ixelles, a
suburb of Brussels. At the age of seventeen he decided to study
for the priesthood and was sent to the Gregorian University in
Rome. He was ordained a priest on September 4, 1927. When
he returned to Belgium in 1929, he taught for a while at the
secondary school where he had been a student, and then at the
minor seminary of Malines. In August, 1940, he was appointed
vice rector of the Catholic University of Louvain. When the
rector of the university was put in jail by the Nazis, the young
vice rector took up the burdens of the office. Eventually his
name was put on a list of thirty hostages that the Germans intended to execute. The Allied liberation of Belgium saved his

life. On November 12, 1945, he was appointed auxiliary bishop
to Cardinal Van Roey, Archbishop of Malines. When Cardinal
Van Roey died, in August, 1961, the name of the see was changed
from Malines to Malines-Brussels, and Bishop Suenens was named
to head the archdiocese.

He has been an archbishop only since December 15, 1961,
and a cardinal only since March 19, 1962, but this 59-year-old
prelate has achieved things that few, if any, of his predecessors
could match. Pope John named him to the Commission on
Diocesan Government in preparation for the Second Vatican
Council, then to the Secretariat for Extraordinary Affairs at
the Council, and finally to the Coordinating Commission of
seven cardinals, on whose work so much depends for successful
completion of the Council.

When the cardinal told me, in the interview which follows,
what the theme of the Council would be, I congratulated him,
for I knew that it was the theme he had been working to have
adopted. Very modestly, he said: "Oh, but this was an idea that
His Holiness himself put forward in one of his discourses before
the Council began."

Modesty, gravity and scholarly bearing distinguish this tall,
graying, fatherly prelate. And it is obvious—though he does not
say a word about it—that he has dedicated himself to the sim-
plicity of earlier Christian times. Before I met him, I heard
he had given more than a dozen talks to priests and people
throughout his archdiocese after his return from the first session
of the Council, and at all of them he had appeared in a plain
black cassock with only his pectoral cross and ring to indicate
his episcopal rank. That was how he was dressed when I visited
him.

Beyond the old, picturesque part of town in which he lives,
there are miles of factories. The cardinal's thoughts, it is clear
from his written works, are never far from the people who
work in those factories and the men and women who dedicate
their lives to those people—priests, brothers and sisters, and the
laity who share in their mission. He feels strongly that, as a

bishop, he has been entrusted with the spreading of the Christian message, and that, therefore, the people have need of hearing him. He sees his role as one of service, but it is service given in answer to a need.

QUESTION

Would you tell us, Your Eminence, how the first session of the Council looks to you now?

CARDINAL SUENENS

In making an appraisal of how things went, I would say it is very important to remember two discourses that Pope John gave, one on September 11, before the Council began, and the other on October 11, the opening day of the Council. Perhaps not enough attention was paid to the Pope's September discourse. Actually, it gave the program of the Council in a nutshell. The second discourse gave us our method, with its stress on the positive rather than the negative; it was to be a council of pastoral perspective rather than of juridical condemnations, etc.

When we began our work, we found ourselves confronted with *schemata* that were very juridical in content and in tone. We lost a lot of time pruning this away. Things went slowly at first, but there was a grace of the Holy Spirit operating all the while in the fact that the bishops were able to get to know each other. It meant an enrichment of the life of the Church, and that is important. In the next session of the Council, there should be even more opportunity for these meetings and discussions between bishops. As everybody knows, we have the coffee bar, but that is not enough.

It was providential that we began with the discussion on the liturgy. It was one of the better prepared *schemata*. We soon got down to the vital problem of how to define the truth in a language or terminology appropriate to our times. The pastoral view, it was seen, had to be preferred over the juridical and scholastic approach. Some of the bishops, of course, as theologians, were more keen on the doctrinal and juridical approach, but they came around to seeing the necessity of the pastoral approach.

QUESTION

Could you tell us something about preparations for the next session of the Council?

CARDINAL SUENENS

We had to boil down all the material, of course. Otherwise, the Council would have been longer than Trent. The Coordinating Commission, to which I was appointed, met January 21-28. The *schemata* were divided out among the seven cardinals of the commission. We met at Cardinal Cicognani's place in the Vatican, and by the end of the seven days we had all completed our revision of the *schemata* entrusted to us. We unanimously accepted the work of each cardinal. Substantial progress was made here.

Incidentally, there has been a common mistake in the press about the *schemata*. One reads all the time that there were seventy or more *schemata* that had to be boiled down to twenty. Actually, there were not seventy *schemata*. There were seventy or more fascicles, but in some cases there were a number of fascicles for one *schema*.

The Holy Father approved the work of our commission, and he called the heads of the various Council commissions together for a meeting with us. We transmitted to them the directives we had worked out for the new revision of the schemata.

QUESTION

Is it true that a theme has been adopted for the Council?

CARDINAL SUENENS

Yes. It was decided that the central theme would be *Ecclesia Christi, Lumen Gentium* (Church of Christ, Light of the

Nations). The first part of this theme title (*Ecclesia Christi*) would cover the Church in its internal aspect (*ad intra*), and the second part (*Lumen Gentium*) would cover its external aspect (*ad extra*). The *schemata* under the first part have the titles they already had, but for the second part we will use the heading *Praesentia Ecclesiae in Mundo Hodierno* (The Church's Presence in the Modern World). It is in this part that we will work out something on the dignity of the human person, family problems, economic questions and social justice, and the international field. Some new mixed commissions will have to be formed to deal with some of the questions under the new second heading. The members of the Coordinating Commission will return to Rome in March to follow up on the progress that will have been made.

QUESTION

Could Your Eminence tell us what schemata you worked on?

CARDINAL SUENENS

Yes. I was entrusted with the tract on the Church, the one on the Blessed Virgin Mary, and the three that cover the moral, social and international orders.

QUESTION

Your Eminence is well known for books, pastoral letters and years of study in religious sociology. It is likely that you have special hopes and expectations from the Council along these lines. Could you tell us something about them?

CARDINAL SUENENS

Not long ago, on a TV program here in Belgium, I was asked what I thought was the chief problem confronting the Church. I said then, and I still say, the problem is to change passive Catholics into active ones. Part of the problem is how to convey to the people that as baptized members of Christ they must be apostles. It is commonly said that the sphere of temporal affairs is the special province of the laity. I think this is a mistake. The laity have a special role to play in the temporal sphere, but they also have a role in the spiritual area. They are members not only of the City of Man but of the City of God. They are definitely to share in the work of the expansion of the Church. In the spiritual area they are to work with priests, of course, but the point is that they are to work in this area.

We must find a way of teaching this idea. A first step, of course, would be to revise the catechism, so that, for example, the first question ("Why did God make you?") would not be answered simply, "to know Him, to love Him and to serve Him," but "to know Him and to help in making Him known; to love Him and to help in making Him loved; to serve Him and to help in bringing others to His service."

Our whole system of education must be revised and adapted to that approach, from the earliest grades up. There is a lot of theoretical talk about this, but we haven't yet got a program of training going that carries it out. We have to bring this idea to our children and students at all levels. Also, we have to give them a choice as to what form their help in this sharing of the apostolate will take. We have to give the children actual, concrete things to do. It is my hope and dream that as a result of this change in our educational system we will produce adult Catholics who accept their full responsibility, even to the extent that every Catholic will be out spreading the word, the Good News, and making converts. Could we hope, perhaps, that every Catholic would eventually be making five converts? That would mean the conversion of the world, considering Catholics in proportion to the world's population.

A major question for the Council, I think, will be what to say about the Christian family. One of the big obstacles to the Christianization of society is the inadequate sexual education that we have become used to. Too much has been left to the instinct of the people in this matter. We need more research about fertility and all the topics of married life, and we have to communicate the results to married people. As you may know, I have sponsored international congresses at Louvain for this purpose, and the fifth one will be held this year. I think that the Second Vatican Council should legislate a period of two or three months' special preparation for people who are intending to marry. In other words, I think something like the work of the Cana movement should be made obligatory. We have six years of preparation for the priesthood, and two years of preparation for Holy Communion. Why not similar preparation for the sacrament of matrimony, with frank conferences in which priest, future spouses and experts on various topics would collaborate?

Moving up to discussion of the next stratum in the Church, the religious, I find it convenient to liken them to noncommissioned officers in the army. In this comparison, the officers would be the priests, and the laity would be the soldiers. But when I say "religious" here I mean to include all those in the Church who lead lives of total dedication, including members of secular institutes. There are about a million people in this category in the Church today. What a potential there is here! Just as a priest gives the spirit to the work of the laity in this or that area, why shouldn't religious do likewise? In my new book, *Promotion apostolique de la religieuse,* I propose that Sisters should have such a function with regard to women. And more than that. I say that a Sister teaching catechism is a good thing, but it is far better if she teaches a group and then sends each of them out to do the teaching.

QUESTION

There has been considerable discussion about your book, which has appeared in English under the title The Nun in the World. *Is it true that you sent a copy of the book to every bishop in the world?*

CARDINAL SUENENS

Yes, I did. I arranged that the book should be published in seven languages, and I sent a copy to each bishop in his own language, or in the one of these seven he was most familiar with. At one point in the book I explicitly ask the Fathers of the Council for an affirmation in principle of the new role of women religious as *animatrices* (spiritual guides) of women among the laity, and I ask that directives be given to ensure that the constitutions of orders and congregations have nothing in them that would impede this role. The book was written with the female religious chiefly in mind, but much of the book can be applied to male religious and to the training of priests in seminaries.

QUESTION

How would this matter be managed with regard to seminaries?

CARDINAL SUENENS

I think the Council should stress the need of apostolic formation in the seminaries. We are still living with the Council of Trent's idea of seminaries. The stress is on spiritual and intellectual formation, but there is really nothing on practical apostolic training. It is a temptation for many to solve the problem by simply adding a year of pastoral studies to the seminary course. I say no; that is not the way to do it. All six years of the seminary course must be organized so that this pastoral training becomes an integral part of the whole course. One of the main things a priest must learn is how to get other people to do the work of the apostolate in various areas. I have been thinking along these lines for some time now. You can read a good account of how I would like this pastoral training worked into seminary education in *Le Christ au monde*, an international review of apostolic experiences, which has an English edition. I asked Father Jean Lefebvre to write that article in the third issue of 1961. It is an essay on direct formation for the apostolate in a seminary.

QUESTION

Can you say something about possible connections of the Council's work with the movement toward Christian unity?

CARDINAL SUENENS

I am sure that the next session of the Council will see a study of the relationship between the Pope and the bishops. I hope that the definition of papal infallibility which was made at the First Vatican Council will be re-presented in a manner that will remove many misunderstandings on the part of Protestants and members of the Orthodox churches. We must stress the collegiality of the bishops, the fact that the college of bishops is a body of bishops descended from the twelve Apostles united under the leadership of Peter and his successors. By our attention to the fact of the collegiality of the bishops, we will show the Orthodox that we are thinking along a line that means so much to them. Moreover, by stressing the role of the laity in the Church, we will reassure the Protestants that we hold something very dear to them—the sharing of the people in the royal priesthood of Christ. Thus, the Second Vatican Council will be an act of charity to our separated brethren—Orthodox, Anglicans and Protestants— just as it will be an act of charity to Catholics in its return to the purity of the Gospel message.

The cardinal invited me to stay for dinner after my interview with him. In turned out to be a dinner for all of his vicars. The cardinal has divided his archdiocese into four "pastoral zones," with a vicar general for each who has responsibilities a bishop would normally exercise, e.g., creation of new parishes, construction of new churches, building of schools, inspection of institutions, coordination of activities. One or other of the vicars is also archdiocesan director in a special field (e.g., the vicar of the Brussels zone is in charge of the archdiocesan school system), and there is a monsignor at the top of the whole pastoral setup for coordination of the work of the four vicars. One of the vicars is an auxiliary bishop. I noticed that he was dressed exactly like the cardinal—black cassock and black sash, with no trace of red—and I noticed that all of the vicars seemed to be about forty years old, except, perhaps, the bishop, whose gray hair makes him look a little older. It soon became evident to me that the cardinal had assembled a team that has youthful vigor, competence and complete commitment to ideals he had touched upon in the interview with me.

By his arrangement of pastoral zones and vicars (in addition to the vicar general in the present canonical sense), the cardinal has succeeded in elevating pastoral above administrative cares in his archdiocese. The arrangement is being studied by many other Fathers of the Second Vatican Council.

IV

PROCEEDING

WITH CONFIDENCE

The parish of St. André in Lille, France, has the remarkable distinction of having produced both the President of France and the dean of the cardinals of France. Achille Cardinal Liénart, Bishop of Lille, a president of the Second Vatican Council and a member of the important Coordinating Commission, was born in the parish of St. André on February 7, 1884. Charles de Gaulle was born a few years later and a few streets away. It was with obvious joy that Cardinal Liénart told me about the day Charles de Gaulle returned as President to the parish church where they had both been baptized. The cardinal received the President in the sanctuary, where he had come to assist at Mass.

The church is on the Rue Royale that Louis XIV laid out straight as an arrow, and it is only a short walk along the street to the Bishop's House. The cardinal's birthplace, on a street just off the Rue Royale, faces a side entrance of the Bishop's House which leads into the chancery offices. When Achille Liénart was born, the son of a manufacturer, the big place across the street was a hotel and the Diocese of Lille did not exist. Lille was in the Archdiocese of Cambrai. It was thirty years later, in 1913, that the Diocese of Lille was created and the hotel converted into a bishop's residence. Cardinal Liénart is only the third Bishop of Lille.

Both Achille Liénart and Charles de Gaulle were students at

[43]

the Jesuit College of St. Joseph in Lille. The future cardinal then went to the Seminary of St. Sulpice in Paris, where he was ordained to the priesthood on June 29, 1907. Later, at the Institut Catholique in Paris, he earned a *licence* in letters; a doctorate in theology, in Rome; a degree in biblical studies at the Pontifical Biblical Institute, in Rome. He returned to France to teach Sacred Scripture at the major seminary of the Cambrai Archdiocese.

When World War I broke out, Father Liénart volunteered as a chaplain. He was wounded twice and was awarded the Legion of Honor and the *croix de guerre* with six citations. One of these citations was given for his heroism during a French retreat at the time of the fighting around Soissons. He crossed the river Aisne alone under enemy fire many times in a rowboat to bring wounded French soldiers, one by one, across the river. After the war he returned to teaching, at the new major seminary of the Diocese of Lille. Seven years later, he became pastor of St. Christopher's Parish at Tourcoing. Two years later, on October 6, 1928, Pope Pius XI appointed him Bishop of Lille. He soon built a new seminary, began a new cathedral, and called a synod to draw up the first statutes of the diocese.

From the very beginning, Bishop Liénart worked for improvement of workers' conditions. In 1929 he secured from the Holy See the famous instruction of the Sacred Congregation of the Council on the right and duty of Catholic workers to join a union. He mediated strikes, fought the influence of the right-wing Action Française over students in his diocese, condemned both Communism and the "economic liberalism that has corrupted capitalism and led to its abuses." At the consistory of June 30, 1930, Pope Pius XI proclaimed him a cardinal.

Cardinal Liénart stood up to the Nazis during the occupation of his diocese in World War II. The German-controlled press reported that he supported the Nazi policy of deporting Frenchmen to Germany for forced labor. His vigorous and public denial, given in an address to seven thousand youths, resulted in Nazi charges that he was a "Gaullist" and should be arrested for "encouraging youths to shirk their duty," but he was never jailed. When SS troops massacred eighty-five residents of Ascq, including the pastor, the cardinal came to a memorial Mass for the victims and said: "We cannot let the curtain of forgetfulness fall on a crime like that. . . . Our sense of justice calls out not for vengeance but for punishment of the guilty."

Since the war, the cardinal has spoken out on many major issues: in 1949, against cooperation with Communists; in 1954, on the priest-worker controversy; in 1960, against anti-Semitism and race prejudice. In 1954, he was named Prelate of the Prelacy Nullius of the Mission of France, with headquarters at Pontigny. This home-mission movement had been organized in 1941, but, as the cardinal explains in the following interview, the work did not go well until the 1954 arrangement was made. The new, nationwide canonical jurisdiction given by Pope Pius XII freed the movement from various diocesan complications.

Judging from his extraordinary record as a chaplain in World War I, and from the vigor he showed at the first session of the Second Vatican Council, I expected to find that Cardinal Liénart was like a lion, but he turned out to be one of the gentlest and kindest men I have ever met. He is now in his eightieth year, but he is tall and straight, and he seems much less than seventy years old.

The cardinal was preparing a pastoral letter on the Second Vatican Council for the people of his diocese when I visited him. When I suggested that the cardinal take the opportunity to communicate his ideas to the people of America also, he replied: "I do not want to give the appearance of being a leader or molder of opinion at the Council. It is true that, because I spoke first at the Council, I have been given a larger role to play than I expected. But I want to be a bishop among the bishops. I will talk to you as I would talk to my own people, and if you wish, you may communicate that to your readers."

The cardinal said that his main preoccupation was the same as the Holy Father's, *aggiornamento*—presentation of the Church's message to the modern world in language readily intelligible to modern man. At the beginning of his pastoral letter, the cardinal was planning to say something about the question of the collegiality of the bishops, but he would not use that word in the letter because it was too abstract, too technical. It was important from an ecumenical point of view, he said, that the Council should define something about the collegiality of bishops, as well as from the bishops' own point of view, because the role and powers of bishops meant so much to the Orthodox.

Cardinal Liénart told me that over the past ten years he has received Orthodox priests and archimandrites at his seminary for special studies in theology. They have lived at the seminary, and they have sometimes attended the liturgical functions in the seminary chapel. Their presence, he said, has created better mutual understanding and greater esteem on both sides. Some of these archimandrites have become bishops in their native lands.

One of the Orthodox priests had sent the cardinal a little box of incense from a monastery on Mount Athos with the request that the incense be used in the Cathedral of Lille on Holy Thursday, "in order that the prayers of Orthodox and Catholic might rise up to heaven together." The cardinal told me: "I have never had occasion to regret these associations with the Orthodox. Their presence among us has enabled us to share in the experience of suffering that is proper to the condition of being separated."

The cardinal stressed that he and his priests and seminarians could deal confidently with the Orthodox because they could rely on the strength of their Catholic faith. In the same spirit, he said, he had approved and encouraged meetings between his priests and Protestant ministers over the past dozen years or so. He agreed that there was also a role for the laity to play in this dialogue, but it took special preparation. The cardinal said there was something like the American National Conference of Christians and Jews in France, *Amitié Judéo-Chrétienne*. He quite willingly endorsed the good aims of this work. With regard to Jews, he said: "I am very sorry to see the revival of anti-Semitism that has cropped up in some places. As you may know,

I wrote a pastoral letter against anti-Semitism two years ago. I stand by that statement and I reassert it." The cardinal stated: "As I said in that letter, we must defend ourselves against the idea so often imputed to us—and so simplistic—that the Jewish people became a people cursed by God since the time when, through its leaders, it rejected the promised Messiah, in the person of Jesus, and that the Jewish people became a deicide people when it brought the Son of God to His death on the Cross. That idea has spawned the conclusion that the Jewish people deserved the contempt and hostility of Christ's true disciples. It is only a short step, then, to the idea that everything is legitimate to make the Jewish people pay for their crime.

"The true doctrine of the Church is quite different, and the attitude that the Church would have us take toward the Jewish people is the opposite of that spirit of reprisal.

"It is not true that the Jewish people were first or alone in responsibility for the death of Jesus. The true cause of His death on the Cross is to be found in the sins of men, and therefore we are all responsible for His death. The Jews were only the executors of the act for which we are responsible.

"Nor is it true that the Jews are a deicide people, for, if they had been aware of His divinity, they would have believed in Him and would not have brought about His death. Their unawareness of His divinity resulted in their being given the forgiving word of Jesus Himself: 'Father, forgive them, for they do not know what they are doing.' That forgiveness was proclaimed by the Apostles, in the presence of the people of Jerusalem. We read in the Acts of the Apostles (3:14-15, 17-19) that St. Peter said to them in one of his first discourses after Pentecost: 'You disowned the Holy and Just One . . . the author of life you killed . . . And now, brethren, I know that *you acted in ignorance, as did also your rulers.* But in this way God fulfilled what he had announced beforehand by the mouth of all the prophets, namely, that his Christ should suffer. Repent, therefore, and be converted, that your sins may be blotted out . . .'

"It is important to stress," the cardinal said, "that in our dealings with Protestants and Jews and all others in the modern pluralistic society we should proceed with confidence. If we really trust in the faith we have, we can penetrate the society around us without fear, taking our full share in the life of the world and, at the same time, being a leaven in the life of that world. This should be true not only of priests and religious and members of secular institutes, but also, especially, of the graduates of our Catholic schools."

The cardinal can speak with special competence about this subject, for he is chairman of the committee of bishops that directs the Mission of France. "This attempt to reach the masses of nonpracticing Catholics," the cardinal said, "has been meeting with considerable success now that it has passed through the difficult period of some years back, when it did not have a completely clear juridical status. Once Pope Pius XII gave the Mission of France a clear canonical status and constitution, the work went forward with vigor." The flow of vocations for this special work has pleased the cardinal. He says he now has about three hundred priests in the work, and some are working also in French-speaking parts of Africa. Requests for some of these priests have come from bishops in Latin America, and the cardinal has begun to answer some of those requests.

The cardinal's experiences as head of the Mission of France give special force to his statement that the Second Vatican Council is meeting at a time of crisis for the Church: "Yes, there is a crisis. If we do not take steps to do more about achieving *rapprochement* between the Church and the modern world, we are in danger of finding ourselves considered unrealistic and irrelevant." The cardinal said: "Outside the Church a world has been born that is so fascinated by the progress of science it forgets that science only discovers the marvels of nature created by God. This world wants to build a universe without God, a material universe where it thinks it can find happiness. This is the world that the Church must reach with its message that the destiny God intends for the world is infinitely higher and more beautiful.

"The Church simply must make its message intelligible to this world," the cardinal insisted. "The Church must make her message of truth convincing to the modern world. We have to take steps that the world will listen and that our contemporaries may receive the grace of participating in the divine life of the Church."

In this connection, the cardinal said he expected the Second Vatican Council would deal with some of the major issues of the times, for example, the questions of war, peace, and hunger. He said it was planned that topics of social action would be treated under the headings of the apostolate, the family and the international field. How would the topics be treated? The cardinal said he thought there would be statements of principles, rather than a detailing of practical steps to be taken. In the statement of principles the Council would confront the problems of the modern world with the true spirit of Christ and with the relevant content of the Church's teaching.

Throughout its work, the Council would have in mind that its object is the Church and how the Church can better fulfill its mission to all men and all peoples. "Bishops, priests and people, we are all invited to share in this work of renewal," the cardinal said, "not only according to personal ideas, which are always too narrow, but according to the designs of God. We must begin, then, to acquire a true awareness of what our Church is and the fullness of the work that it should accomplish.

"The Church," the cardinal continued, "has too often been visualized as a big administrative affair, with a central power at Rome and diocesan subdivisions with a bishop at the head who is some kind of functionary. True," he said, "the Church has an administration, and has to have one as a society, but the Church is much more. It is a living body, with members closely linked to the head, the risen Christ, represented in visible manner on earth by the successor of St. Peter. And the bishops are precisely the living link by which priests and faithful throughout the world are in vital union with Christ.

"The Council," the cardinal said, "makes us see an aspect of our Church that we have been too little aware of. We have always known that the Pope, successor of St. Peter, is, in accordance with the will of our Lord Himself, the supreme authority of the whole Church. We have been less aware of the fact that the bishops are also responsible for the Church before God together with the Pope."

The cardinal explained: "We have become used to considering the bishop above all as the local authority of a diocese—in communion with the Pope, of course, but charged only with a little portion of the Church. One effect of our gathering together in Rome was that we realized vividly what a spiritual bond unites us, and what a general responsibility we share in common as successors of the community of twelve Apostles to which our Lord confided His Church at the same time that He confided it to Peter.

"Thus this truth came fully to light in our consciousness," the cardinal continued, "that if each of us was the head of a particular diocese, our episcopate conferred on us also the duty of participating collectively, in union with the Pope, in the direction of the doctrinal and pastoral work of the Church throughout the world. The Holy Father himself drew us on in this consideration. He left us completely free to express our opinions on matters of doctrine, discipline and the apostolate with which we were preoccupied at the time. He left us free in coming to decisions about these matters—decisions that we would agree upon with him. He asked us to help him in giving our ancient Church a new youth by tempering it again in its sources. He asked us to help him manifest the Church in all its purity to our separated brethren, in order, as far as possible, to remove the obstacles that still prevent the fulfillment of our Lord's final prayer concerning those who believe in Him: 'That all may be one, even as thou, Father, in me and I in thee.' The Holy Father asked us to study with him how to present to the world, as it is today, the message of hope and salvation entrusted to the Church. We had to find a way of presenting it that would do a better job of meeting the modern world's needs and expectations.

"Of course," the cardinal added, "this was exceptional. A council is a rare event. It is only at great intervals that the bishops have occasion to exercise their collective responsibility under this solemn form. Nevertheless, this common responsibility belongs to them always, for it is inherent in their title of successors of the Apostles. On them today, as on the Apostles at the beginning, the whole Church of Jesus Christ rests. This wonderful realization should certainly enlarge the idea we have of the church—yes, indeed, in a remarkable way.

"Yes," the cardinal continued, "the Council has given all of us—bishops, priests and people—an opportunity to become aware that we are the Church, and to become aware of the extent of our responsibilities in the context of the world in which we find ourselves. The Council gives us the opportunity to do away with ideas that are too human and too narrow—all too often we find ourselves entangled in them—and to shake off routine, habitual ways of doing things. The Council brings to our souls, like a new breath of the Holy Spirit, the idea that, as the Holy Father has desired, we should restore to our Church its true countenance in all its purity and its universal radiance in all its vigor.

"Our cooperation in this effort," the cardinal pointed out, "is, in fact, indispensable. We are the Church of the twentieth century. In order that the Church bring herself up to date, we must accept the changes and adaptations that the Council will judge necessary for spreading the Good News of the Gospel throughout the world. We must enter resolutely on the path that the Council traces out for us."

The cardinal then gave some practical considerations that he intended to include in the pastoral letter he was preparing for the people of his own diocese: "There are a number of things in which we should change our way of doing things, and that could be an unpleasant experience for us. But the point here is that we are not out to please ourselves. Our task is not to keep for ourselves the gifts of God that we enjoy. The point is that, for the Church and therefore for ourselves, we should be doing everything to communicate those gifts to all men, who are our brothers.

"There will be, for example, some changes in our liturgical functions, in order that the initiated will not be the only ones to understand the liturgy but that it may become more accessible to everyone. Also, the Christian community will be invited to take an active part in the liturgy, in order that to our acts of personal devotion we may add the collective prayer of the people of God, which we are. This bringing up to date of our liturgical life has already been started among my people, and it is going well, but we must make it the general practice everywhere in order to enter fully into the Church's prospects.

"A change of spirit, still more profound than what we now know, will be asked of us with regard to Christians who are separated from us—Orthodox, Anglicans, Protestants. These are no longer the times of the sorrowful religious wars. We live no longer in an age of doctrinal controversies. Our separated brethren, like ourselves, aspire to rediscover the unity they lost, and our Church, preserving intact the revealed doctrine entrusted to her, asks us—all of us—to show our separated brethren sentiments of sincere, brotherly charity. The Church asks all of us to work with her to prepare for the reconciliation of all those who believe in Jesus Christ, and to prepare for the reestablishment of their visible unity. It is such an important matter that our Holy Father Pope John XXIII has not hesitated to say that God will judge us on what we will have done or what we will have neglected to do to help Christian unity. Every one of us, therefore, should take this task seriously and show himself open to this new spirit.

"The same point is to be made with regard to the world in which we find ourselves. It is not our function to condemn the world for its errors or its impiety; our mission is to save the world. For that mission of saving, we should love the world, with a universal love, extending to all men and all peoples, just as the charity of Jesus Christ extends to all men and all peoples.

"There is the true visage of the Church. That is the image of the Church that we should manifest to the modern world in everything we do, in order that the modern world may receive the Church's message and be saved.

"If the modern world is going to believe and be saved, it must see everywhere that the bishops, priests, religious and Christian people engaged in its service are aware of all its sufferings and all its worries—hunger, war, social injustices. The modern world must see bishops, clergy and laity working everywhere to defend the inalienable rights of the family, social justice, international peace—and all this precisely in the name of Christian morality.

"In the light of the Council, the Church appears more alive than ever and, in fact, emerges as the true hope of the world. Every one of us, therefore, must be aware of his responsibility in everything he does. Every one of us must do what depends on him, according to the place Divine Providence has given him in order that his cooperation may be contributed to the great work. Let us be sowers of the good grain of the Gospel in the Church, and God will see to the ripening of the harvest."

After the interview, before I could stop him, the cardinal picked up a large coffee table and carried it across the room, in order that I might type on it in the better light near a large window that looked out on a pleasant garden. In his kindness he had also arranged that Monsignor P. Glorieux would join us for lunch. Monsignor Glorieux was rector of the Catholic University of Lille when the cardinal asked him to come to the Bishop's House as secretary. The cardinal introduced the monsignor to me with the words: "Here is my collaborator in my work for the Council." Later, after I had finished typing out the text of the interview, Monsignor Glorieux accompanied me along the Rue Royale. I observed that the cardinal's pastoral letter would be a very beautiful and very important text, and that the cardinal was fortunate to have a theologian like Monsignor Glorieux to produce such documents for him. "Oh," he replied, "but the cardinal himself is writing that letter. I have helped him on Council work, but he writes his pastoral letters. And why not, eh?" Indeed yes, I agreed, as I recalled the cardinal's degrees, his years of teaching and his years of experience. The cardinal has for many years been much more than an honorary member of the Sacred Congregation of the Council, the Sacred Congregation of Seminaries and Universities, and the Pontifical Commission of Biblical Studies. All of this underlined the importance of what he had said about the Jewish question and about Christian unity.

V

TRUTH

FIRST AND ALWAYS

Giuseppe Cardinal Siri, Archbishop of Genoa and president of the Italian Bishops' Conference, was grave and thoughtful the day I visited him. The day before, he told me, he had been surprised to discover in an Italian newspaper an account of a speech he had delivered during the first session of the Council. "I did not give out that text," the cardinal said, "but obviously the writer had a copy of it. Someone violated the secrecy of the Council in giving it to him." In making judgments about the speech, the cardinal added, the writer acted "in a singularly improper manner, in view of the fact that the Fathers of the Council themselves do not pass judgments on one another's speeches."

The cardinal looks like one of the nobles in the many paintings that hang on the walls of his palace next to the Cathedral of San Lorenzo in Genoa, and the incident of the pirated speech showed that he had the manner of a noble, although he is actually the son of working-class parents.

Slim, bespectacled, still dark-haired at the age of fifty-seven, the cardinal gives an impression of vitality, keen intelligence and intense seriousness. I knew that he had become a priest at the unusually early age of twenty-two, and had won a doctorate in theology the following year at the Gregorian University, the only member of the class to do it with full points. He was a theology professor at twenty-four, a bishop at thirty-seven and a cardinal at forty-six. He has written books about social problems, as well as theology textbooks, and I have heard it said that he has settled more labor disputes, as an arbitrator, than any other man in Italy. Cardinal Siri served as a member of the Central Preparatory Commission of the Second Vatican Council.

It was good to learn that this brilliant and forceful molder of opinion in the Italian Church had a sense of humor. It came out when he told me how much he relished something that Cardinal Léger, Archbishop of Montreal, whispered to him as they walked together in procession on December 9 at the beginning of that day's canonization ceremonies. It was the day after the first session of the Council ended. Many of the bishops had gone home. Those in attendance were up at the front near the altar of St. Peter's, and the rest of the tiers of Council Fathers' seats had been given to seminarians. As they passed the seminarians, Cardinal Léger whispered to Cardinal Siri: "Look—the Third Vatican Council!" Cardinal Siri's smile grew wider as he recalled how he noticed that the seminarians Cardinal Léger was pointing to were from his own seminary of Genoa; they were there because one of the day's three new saints came from Genoa.

The day I visited Cardinal Siri was the seventeenth anniversary of the death of Pietro Cardinal Boetto, his predecessor as Archbishop of Genoa and Cardinal Bea's predecessor as a Jesuit member of the Sacred College. There was a picture of Cardinal Boetto on the table beside Cardinal Siri. He told me what a great and lovable man the cardinal had been. In this, and in everything else he said, it was obvious that Cardinal Siri was a man of great loyalty and devotion to men he esteems and to causes in which he believes.

QUESTION

In an overall view of the Second Vatican Council's first session, what does Your Eminence see as its achievements?

CARDINAL SIRI

It may take fifty years before the full achievements of the Council are discerned. But certain fruits are evident already, and they are important. First, the Church sees more clearly now the work that is cut out for it for the next hundred years. And, as the Holy Father himself has indicated, the approach is a pastoral one. But it is obvious to me that some have misunderstood what is meant by the pastoral approach. They seem to think of it in negative rather than in positive terms. It was a wise and provident thing that we began the work of the Council with attention to the liturgy. It struck a very positive note. It went to the heart of things. After all, the worship of God is our primary and basic function as true members of the Church. It was also providential that we took up the matter of the unity of all Christians and all men. It is another fruit of the Council that the Church was seen to be deeply concerned about this matter.

Another fruit of the Council, as I see it, is that the Church is presented as primarily and basically concerned with the truth. We have a deposit of faith entrusted to us by our Lord Himself. It is this that we must preserve, protect and preach. It is this that we must be concerned about more than anything else. There are some people in the Church who apparently would push on into certain areas of activity without sufficient consideration for preservation of the truth entrusted to us. The Fathers of the Council know that this would be rash, and their preoccupation with the truth—the truth first and always—makes it evident to those observing the work of the Council that this is the proper procedure. We know, of course, that the truth should be spoken in a way that will help the pastoral aims of the Council. This awareness of the Church's dedication to the truth is an important fruit of the Council. No one should have been surprised that differences of opinion were expressed by the Fathers of the Council. Anyone who knows anything about the Councils of the Church knows that always happens. But the thing to note is the stress on *truth*.

QUESTION

What do you regard as necessary and essential for the success of the next session of the Council?

CARDINAL SIRI

First, it is necessary to reduce the number of topics. Otherwise it will take us many years to finish. Secondly, I wish to stress that those who write about the Council should not prejudge it. If the next session is to do its work well and be received well, we should not be hampered by books and articles that talk too much about what the Council should do or say. If expectations are built up by that kind of writing, and then are not fulfilled, people will think the Council has not succeeded or done its work well.

In connection with this matter of writings about the Council, I should like to point out that there are a number of books today which present studies on religious topics in a manner quite foreign to sound principles of scholarship. I was a professor of theology for many years, and I must say that some of these modern authors need a course in the correct principles of historical study. I am thinking of some of the current writing about Sacred Scripture, for example. Only those who understand the principles of internal and external criticism, and know their limitations, can write accurately on such subjects. It does not help the work of the Church when some modern authors advance mere hypotheses that are without foundation and proceed to come to a conclusion and present a thesis. These so-called modern authors are actually violating the true principles of modern scientific procedure.

For the success of the Council, it is very necessary that we have a supernatural view of it. We must go about our work in accordance with what the Holy Spirit gives us. The Holy Spirit certainly is working in the Council. On a number of occasions I have said to myself: "There is the work of the Holy Spirit." I cannot tell you what those occasions were, for I am bound by the secret of the Council. But I have written down a full account of the Council as I saw it. It is in the archives of my house, to be kept until after I have passed on.

The Holy Father himself asked me to compose such an account.

QUESTION

Does Your Eminence have some special interests that you would like to see the Council consider?

CARDINAL SIRI

Yes. I very much wish to see the Council come to the completion of its work. I am especially interested in seeing a matter brought up at this Council, and I would like to see it made quite clear. I refer to the office and powers of bishops. Why do I want to see this matter treated by the Council? In order that what is true may be clearly seen as true: that the bishops are the apostolic college and that the Pope is the head of that college, but that the Pope is the Vicar of Christ on earth and would be so even if there were no college of bishops. It will be good to do away with all doubts or equivocations about this matter. It should be made quite clear that the bishops bear a certain relationship to the Pope, and thus together with him they make the pronouncements and laws of a council, but the Pope does not have that relationship with regard to the bishops.

Also, I wish to see the subject of revelation concluded with a definite statement. It seems to me that much of the discussion these days about "two fonts of revelation," or insistence that only the term "revelation" be used in order more accurately to express the idea that there are two channels of revelation, Scripture and tradition—all this is, in my opinion, largely a battle of words, a question of terminology. We should get on to the fact of the divine tradition that has been preserved in the Church.

I think it is very desirable, too, that the complex mystery of the Church should be proposed in the tract *De Ecclesia* ("On the Church").

QUESTION

What do you think the Council might do about social questions and the social teaching of the Church?

CARDINAL SIRI

It seems to me that the Council does not have to make decrees or canons on that subject, because it is so thoroughly treated in the encyclicals of the popes, from Leo XIII's *Rerum Novarum* to Pope John's *Mater et Magistra*. It is all there, and it is expressed so well that, as a bishop, I would say we should urge the study of the encyclicals rather than make a whole presentation of the subject in the Council.

I think it would be very helpful, however, if the Council were to present some messages or statements on certain social questions. These would not be decrees or canons, but they would make a profound impression on people, as the first message or statement of the Council did. It would be very helpful, for example, if the Fathers of the Council would issue statements on peace, war, consideration of underprivileged classes of people, etc. It would help people who face certain problems if the Council were to come out with a statement stressing their rights in their problems—the right to a living wage, for example. The work of charity does not proceed properly until the matter of rights is clearly understood and put into practice.

The interview with Cardinal Siri had begun in Italian, but I soon suggested that my Italian was probably not good enough for an Italian cardinal. Since I could speak Latin much better, I asked if we might continue in that language. *Utique, Pater,* he replied, and he continued fluently in Latin. In the evening, I stood with the cardinal's secretary, Monsignor Bartolomeo Pesce (who looks like the pictures one sees of young John Henry Newman), and the two of us translated into Italian as the cardinal read the English text I had typed out. At the end of each page the cardinal said: *Placet.*

VI

THE CHURCH'S

LAST GREAT OPPORTUNITY

Franziskus Cardinal Koenig, Archbishop of Vienna, looks much younger than his fifty-eight years. The scholarly, bespectacled cardinal is slim and sandy-haired and very mild of manner. When I talked with him, however, at his residence beside the historic Cathedral of St. Stephen in Vienna, I soon discerned what many Fathers of the Council had already learned about Cardinal Koenig. Beneath the youthful appearance and mild manner there is one of the most active and mature minds at work in the Church today.

The future cardinal was born in Rabenstein, Lower Austria, on August 7, 1905. His father died when the boy was very young. His mother made great sacrifices to secure an education for him. After completing secondary studies at the school of the 900-year-old Benedictine abbey at Melk, he continued his studies at the University of Vienna and at the Gregorian University in Rome, where he was ordained to the priesthood on October 27, 1933. He spent the next two years doing advanced work in theology and was awarded a doctorate in 1935. During this period he also studied Sacred Scripture and Oriental languages at the Pontifical Biblical Institute.

From his seminary days, the cardinal has specialized in the study of comparative religion. In Rome, his doctoral thesis was about angels in the Old Testament compared with certain tenets

[61]

of Zoroastrianism. On this foundation of studies about the ancient world, he has built up a knowledge of subsequent forms of religion. His knowledge of the religions of the world is probably not exceeded by that of any other member of the Sacred College.

In addition to his constant study and the writing of books, including an encyclopedia on comparative religion, the cardinal has acquired a remarkable fund of pastoral experiences. In 1936, he returned to his native diocese of Sankt Poelten where he served as assistant pastor in a number of towns. He was then sent to study social sciences at the Catholic University of Lille, France. When he returned to Sankt Poelten to resume duties as an assistant pastor, this time at the cathedral parish, he continued his studies in Eastern languages at the University of Vienna and also took up studies in law. During World War II, Father Koenig taught religion to high-school students and headed the Sankt Poelten diocesan youth organization. Under cover of this work, he organized an anti-Nazi movement among the young people.

After the war, he became a professor of religion at a school in Krems an der Donau and a lector in the department of biblical studies at the University of Vienna. Three years later he received a professorship in moral theology on the Salzburg faculty. He was made coadjutor bishop of Sankt Poelten on June 3, 1952, and he was put in charge of press relations for the Austrian Bishops' Conference. In May, 1956, he was named to succeed Theodor Cardinal Innitzer as Archbishop of Vienna. Two years later, at the consistory of December 15, 1958, he was elevated by Pope John XXIII to the College of Cardinals. The following year the cardinal was named military vicar of Austria's armed forces. He is also the Ordinary of Byzantine Rite Catholics in Austria.

Due to the broad scope of his interests and the profound contributions he makes whenever he speaks out on a topic, Cardinal Koenig has had a "good press" in Europe. Certain human-interest happenings have also made him very popular. There was a great outpouring of sympathy for the cardinal in February, 1960, when he was badly smashed up in an automobile accident in Yugoslavia while he was on the way to the funeral of Aloysius Cardinal Stepinac. The bones of his face were broken in half a dozen places, but everything has healed and there are no after-effects.

The cardinal, a member of the Council's Theological Commission, has more than an academic interest in the subject of Church-State relations. He was instrumental in bringing about settlement of a difficult Church property problem in Austria. He had helped to improve Church relations with the government so much that an agreement was soon reached between Austria and the Holy See about this complicated matter.

The cardinal speaks excellent English, and he is fluent in a dozen languages. His linguistic talents account for some of his great influence at the Council, but his gentle manner has much to do with it, too, as a number of Italian bishops have admitted. As the following interview shows, the cardinal speaks frankly and probes deeply, but always without giving offense.

QUESTION

What does Your Eminence regard as achievements of the first session of the Council?

CARDINAL KOENIG

This Council is quite a new thing in the Church. It is much more universal in its makeup than preceding councils. Another important fact about it is that from the very beginning there was created an atmosphere of freedom of expression.

Some of the Italian newspapers I saw during the first part of the Council spoke a great deal about opposition between blocs—between the Italian bishops and what they called the transalpine bishops, referring to the German-speaking bishops chiefly. They were not accurately reporting the case. It was true that we German-speaking bishops and the other transalpine bishops met together, especially when the question arose of electing members of the different commissions. We were not meeting in opposition to the Italian bishops. In fact, lest there be any such idea, we proceeded to make contacts with members of the Italian hierarchy. I am on quite good terms with the Cardinal Archbishop of Venice and the Cardinal Archbishop of Milan, especially, and others, too, had such friends.

It is true, also, I think, that we German-speaking bishops and other transalpine bishops came to the Council generally more completely prepared than the Italian bishops for the various discussions. A number of them were apparently counting on the strong leadership of the Italian cardinals. Some newspapers made more of these facts than was warranted. I am afraid they were projecting their own ideas rather than what was actually going on.

These meetings of the bishops with each other were an important part of the Council. It was the first time, for example, that the French and German bishops had come into such close and extended contact. This is very important for the future of the Church in a Europe that is coming into closer and closer unity. I think it is a contact that will continue to develop. Certainly the remarkable increase in close relationships established between the bishops of Germany, Austria, Belgium, the Netherlands and Switzerland is something that can prove to be quite beneficial to the Church.

With regard to the American bishops, one has heard it said that they are largely administrators and pastors and that they look very much to Europe for contributions in theological ideas. That was not my impression when I met them at the Council and heard them speak. Some of them spoke quite well and quite clearly in Latin and showed that they had a very good grasp of the ideas under discussion. My impression is that in America priests and bishops have clear ideas about the fundamental themes of the faith which are sometimes dimmed or lost sight of in Europe. I think that some of the writing in European theological journals and some of the teaching in our seminaries become involved in complicated discussions at the expense of clarity about the basic essentials. True, some of the American bishops were shy about speaking in Latin, and they had been many years away from the textbooks, but the American episcopacy communicates a sense of the vitality of Church life in America, and in that the United States is far ahead of Europe. Here in Vienna, I have a serious problem of leakage, and I have alerted all my parish priests to the importance of something that we have lost here but that the Church in America seems to have—contact between priests and people through the visiting of families and homes. I have instructed my priests that they are to visit every home in their parishes.

By the way, I read that article about the Council which appeared in the American magazine *New Yorker*. Someone sent me a copy; otherwise I would not have seen it. I was not happy about that article, nor were some of my friends among the American bishops. It did not give an attitude toward developments that we ourselves had.

Another important fact about the first session was the presence of the observer-delegates. I think their presence was a kind of inspiration to us. Not that it directly affected our discussions in the Council, but it was a kind of abiding influence in our subconscious. I talked with some of them, especially the head of the Taizé community. He told me early in the session that he feared the lengthy discussions would not be as helpful or as productive as one might hope. But, as it turned out, I think those lengthy discussions were quite fruitful. Some bishops had their minds made up on one or another point, and then there would be one of those discussions, and a bishop would admit that he had begun to have some doubts about his particular view on a subject, or that he had changed his mind.

Of course, the impress of the Holy Father upon the Council is a major factor. He has communicated his spirit to it. His mark is upon it.

Another thing that made a special impression upon me was the daily opening of the Council meetings with Mass in so many different rites besides the Latin Rite. It made one realize vividly the universality of the Church. The Mass in so many different languages made one realize the adaptability of the Church and the message of our Lord that is conveyed by the Mass. And always—however the prayers before and after the Consecration might vary in the different rites—always, the words of Consecration remained at the center and the heart of the liturgical action. One thought: indeed our faith is one.

QUESTION

What does Your Eminence regard as essential for the success of the coming session of the Council?

CARDINAL KOENIG

It is very important, I think, that the Holy Father open that session and continue to provide his impress upon it. However, if anything should happen to him and we were to have to elect another pope, I am sure that the Council would have to continue. Any new pope would have to keep the work of the Council going. That first session was so important and established such a trend that it really cannot be changed. The trend and the procedure are clear enough, and they are essential for the success of the next session. The work of the Coordinating Commission between the sessions is also quite important. It must simplify the agenda, chiefly by reducing the number of topics. There is so much of generally accepted Church teaching in the present *schemata* that will have to be pressed out, in order that we may get down to the more essential matters for our times.

QUESTION

Does Your Eminence have some special desires or expectations about what the Council could do?

CARDINAL KOENIG

Yes. For one thing, I should like to see more opportunity given to journalists to cover the meetings of the Council.

Instead of having them going about and picking up what they can outside the sessions, I would favor giving them some access to the meetings. It was not easy for the Vatican Press Office to work out the handling of the Council. The Vatican had never had experience with such a big event. But here is a major opportunity for the Church to make her thoughts known to the world. The more ample the coverage, the better it will be for the Church, I think.

I very much look forward to the completion of the tract *De Ecclesia* in the Council. We began to treat this before the end of the first session. It is a subject that involves discussion of the nature of the Church Militant; something on the members of the Church Militant and the question of the necessity of the Church for salvation; something on the episcopate as the highest grade of the sacrament of orders, and a treatment of the priesthood. The relationship between Pope and bishops would be treated in that discussion. Then, after something about residential bishops, we might get on to treatment of the acquiring of the state of perfection; the laity; the magisterium of the Church; authority and obedience in the Church; relations between Church and State; something on the necessity of preaching the Gospel to all peoples and nations. Finally, we should have something on ecumenism.

These topics are actually the outline of the *schema* on the Church that various groups of bishops are meeting to discuss (as, for example, the meeting of the German-speaking bishops in Munich, February 5-6).

I know that the topic of Church and State is very important, especially in the United States, and I do hope that the Council will produce something helpful on the subject. Whatever may have been the thinking of Church authorities in the past on this subject, we have entered into a new era now. In the past, relations between Church and State and the theological thinking on the subject were largely the product of the local situations. In our era, we can and should work out a mode of operation that corresponds to the realities of the times. These are days of separation of Church and State. Very well, then, let us work with this situation. It does give the Church considerable freedom. I would regret it, however, if this spirit of separation of Church and State were to breed a spirit of indifferentism to religion. We must work it out in our modern society that we preserve both the advantages of separation of Church and State *and* the spirit of religion. In this regard, we may have something to learn from Asia and Africa, where the religious spirit of the people so often pervades their lives, while at the same time they are taking on the advantages of modern forms of government.

Our relationships with people around us of other religious beliefs must certainly express a spirit of tolerance. The days of forced conversions and all that are gone. We have emerged into a period of clearer understanding about freedom of conscience, the dignity of man and human rights. In fact, in order to communicate adequately with the world around us on these very subjects, we have to work out a terminology, a mode of speaking, which will be in the language of the people we want to reach—the language of modern man. Our theological language and our philosophical language—largely in terms of scholasticism—is excellent for the training of our clergy, but for the priest to reach the people around him, especially non-Catholics, there is need of using terms that mean something to modern man. Even our term "natural law" often does not convey to others what we mean by it. Very well, then, let us put it another way—a way that will be significant to modern man. Perhaps we can find a good model in the language of the United Nations Charter and other documents that organizations of the United Nations succeed in producing for the understanding of all men today.

QUESTION

It would help communication between Catholics and non-Catholics, I believe, if we could have a translation of the Bible that would be the same for all. Does Your Eminence think such a common Bible for all Christians is a real possibility?

CARDINAL KOENIG

Yes, I do think so. A common Bible is a real possibility because Catholic and non-Catholic biblical scholars agree more and more about the reading of the ancient texts. The results of historical and archaeological study are accepted by both sides when it is clear that the work involved is very objective, and the effect upon biblical studies is agreeable to both sides when it is clear that a contribution has been made. As a result, we find that we converge upon the same word for expressing the statement of the biblical text. I know that such a common translation, the work of Catholic and Protestant scholars in collaboration, has been achieved in Poland with regard to one of the Gospels, and there are other examples of such activity right across Europe. Provided that the resulting work is carefully examined by a bishop's experts and given the approval of a bishop, I would say that a common translation of the Bible could give the ecumenical movement a great psychological boost, in addition to other practical advantages that such a publication would have (for example, the harmony resulting from having the same numberings of Commandments and Psalms, the same spellings of names, etc.).

QUESTION

Your Eminence has long had an interest in social action and in religious sociology. Do you foresee developments in these areas through the work of the Vatican Council?

CARDINAL KOENIG

Before I became a bishop, I taught courses in comparative religion, and I brought out three volumes on *Christ and the Religions of the World*. Two years ago I visited India, and I hope to return there for the next Eucharistic Congress. In studying about the religions of the various countries of the world, and from what I have seen myself, I know the importance of appreciating other cultures and religions. We in the

Church simply must know more and more about the cultures and religions around us. We must discern the positive values in those cultures and religions. There is no country in the world that is without religion—not even the Soviet Union, despite the efforts of the Communists. Surely the question of adaptation, especially in mission countries, can be helped by the Council. India, for example, is such a religious country, and there are so many good elements of culture and religion there which could be absorbed into the liturgy of the Church. Much the same could be said of countries in Africa.

The world is moving in the direction of more and more unity. The Church must take a part in this movement. In fact, I might say that it is the Church's last great opportunity to be a truly worldwide influence, a truly worldwide Church.

After the interview, Cardinal Koenig invited me to accompany him to a meeting of the German-speaking bishops, to be held in Munich. We talked for eight hours more in his compartment on the train. The Coadjutor Archbishop of Vienna and another bishop were with us; two more bishops had come aboard by the time we reached Linz. For the rest of the trip there was a most interesting discussion about the agenda of the two-day meeting in Munich (about how the whole complex subject of the Church should be handled at the next session of the Council). As the train crossed the border of the Archdiocese of Vienna, one of the other bishops observed that we were moving out of the cardinal's jurisdiction. I then mentioned that, according to present Church law, a cardinal could hear confessions anywhere in the world. I asked His Eminence if he would favor the changing of the law so that every bishop could hear confessions anywhere in the world. I knew that many bishops felt it was only proper that they should have this right, since the bishops are the successors of the Apostles. The cardinal agreed. "May I put Your Eminence's agreement on the record as part of the interview?" I asked. "Yes indeed," he replied.

When we arrived in Munich, Cardinal Koenig found he was

famous in Germany because newspapers had reported everywhere that he had gone skiing with Austrian army chaplains during a meeting he had called as military vicar. The idea of a skiing cardinal had, in fact, captured the imagination of Europeans in general. He will be famous everywhere for it. A story I sent back to the United States about the cardinal's Church-State views came out with this headline (added by the editor) in the Boston *Pilot*: "Vienna's 'Skiing Cardinal' Scans Church-State Horizons."

VII

THE POWER

OF GOD

Laurian Cardinal Rugambwa, Bishop of Bukoba, Tanganyika, was born on July 12, 1912, in Bukongo, Tanganyika Territory, East Africa. His parents, members of the Nsiba tribe, were not Catholics at the time of his birth, but his father was baptized when the boy was seven years old. A year after his father was received into the Church, the boy, who had been attending catechism class at the Kagondo mission of the White Fathers, was baptized with the name Laurian. The date of his baptism was March 13, 1921. Later, his mother and two other children were received into the Church. The family name Rugambwa means "renowned." This new Catholic family certainly would live up to its name, for young Laurian was destined to become the first Negro cardinal of the Church, a member of the Central Preparatory Commission of the Second Vatican Council, and one of the key Fathers of the Council.

The future cardinal completed his early education at Rutabo, under the tutelage of the White Fathers. At the age of fourteen, he entered the minor seminary at Robya (Tanganyika). He continued his studies at the major seminary of Katigondo, Uganda, where his seminary training was conducted by the White Fathers. It was a White Father bishop, Most Reverend Joseph Huwiler, who ordained him to the priesthood on December 12, 1943, at Hutabo mission.

Father Rugambwa spent the next five years in regular parish work among his own people in the Bukoba Vicariate. In 1948, he was sent to Rome for higher studies at the Pontifical Urban College. He received a doctorate in Canon Law *magna cum laude*. He then returned to Tanganyika and, on December 13, 1951, was named Titular Bishop of Febiana and Vicar Apostolic of the newly created Vicariate of Lower Kagera. Bishop Rugambwa was the first African to be raised to the episcopal rank in Tanganyika.

On March 25, 1953, Bishop Rugambwa was transferred to the new Diocese of Rutabo, Tanganyika. As head of the new diocese, he did a great deal to encourage the growth of trade schools and colleges. In 1957, he visited the United States, chiefly to secure help for his schools. Among many happy memories of that trip were an invitation to address the Michigan State Legislature at Lansing, and a visit with Father John LaFarge, associate editor (and editor in chief emeritus) of *America,* whose work for interracial justice had long been admired by the bishop.

At the consistory of March 28, 1960, Pope John proclaimed Bishop Rugambwa a cardinal. Four months later, the cardinal became the head of the new Diocese of Bukoba, which includes his former Diocese of Rutabo. The number of Catholics in the Diocese of Rutabo had increased from 42,000 to nearly 62,000 in his seven years as Ordinary. Now, under the new arrangement, he was the shepherd of 137,000 Catholics in a total population of some 340,000 people.

I first met Cardinal Rugambwa when he came to the United States late in the spring of 1961. Numerous honorary degree ceremonies and other functions were on the agenda of his three-week visit, but he took time out to visit Father LaFarge again at Campion House, residence of the *America* editors. He stayed for dinner with us. Tall, slim and noble of bearing, the cardinal, we soon discerned, was actually a very shy and modest person. In the hours of conversation with him after dinner that day, we came to appreciate the keen intelligence of the cardinal, his interest in educational and social questions particularly, and his constant talent of listening carefully to every man's opinion while (one could see) he made sure and telling judgments on all points made. A little more than a year later, when the Second Vatican Council had begun and the 299 Council Fathers representing Africa were delegating one of their number to speak for them, it was usually Cardinal Rugambwa that they chose. We could well imagine the impression the tall, stately, but ever gentle cardinal made whenever he rose to address the Council.

The remarkable cohesion and effectiveness of those 299 bishops from Africa (sixty-nine of them native-born Africans) was something I wanted to ask the cardinal about when I had the opportunity late in March, 1963. He was staying at the Collegio San Pietro, near the Porta San Pancrazio, while conciliar commissions were meeting in preparation for the second session of the Council. I knew that the Council Fathers of Africa had met in regional conferences every week during the first session of the Council, and that there had been three full assemblies of the Council Fathers from the whole continent of Africa during that first session. Their organization and efficiency were much admired by bishops of other continents. The cardinal gave me the details of the organization that the African bishops had worked out, and he had things to say on several topics that were especially significant coming from him and the African hierarchy, which obviously agreed with him, as was clear from what he said.

I asked the cardinal, first, what had especially impressed him about the first session of the Second Vatican Council. He replied:

I would say that this Ecumenical Council is one of the best manifestations of the power of God. If we consider all the circumstances regarding this Council, we cannot but see the power of God behind it. There is no human power in the history of the whole world that ever convened so many people from every corner of the earth. Not even the United Nations has succeeded in doing what the Second Vatican Council did. No human power ever succeeded in gathering together over three thousand people of different ages, mentalities, backgrounds and languages to discuss important, vital matters with such fraternal charity as has been demonstrated to the world by this Council. An Italian bishop of ninety-nine walked in procession alongside a Peruvian of thirty-four; a bishop from Africa could be seen seated with a European on one side and maybe a Chinese on the other side, while behind him one could see a bearded Oriental bishop flanked by Indian or Japanese bishops. It was indeed the power of God that brought all this about.

With my next question I had in mind a number of facts I had just read in the report "L'Espérance Africaine," in the March 1 issue of *Informations catholiques internationales.* I had read there that the 299 Council Fathers from Africa represented more than 10 percent of the Council, that Africa contained 8.5 percent of the world's population and a little over 4 percent of the world's Catholics. The report stressed that the bishops of Africa knew their people and shared their desire for unity, and this was why they formed a continental episcopal conference built up on twenty national conferences and nine regional conferences. I put my questions this way: "The African bishops certainly impressed everybody, especially in the way they arranged conferences and set up a special Secretariat for the whole continent of Africa. Could you tell us something about that?" The cardinal replied:

The Pan-African Secretariat is an organization of the bishops from Africa taking part in the Second Vatican Council. We felt it was necessary to have such an organization in order to coordinate ideas and experiences of all the Council Fathers from the same continent. We saw it to be as necessary as any other Secretariat or Bishops' Conference. Meeting in Rome for the Council provided us with an opportunity for reunion that would have been much harder to achieve at home. The bishops of other countries felt the same way; many of them were meeting together much more easily than they could have at home. The aim of the Secretariat is to unite all the bishops of Africa for quicker, more coordinated cooperation in the work of the Council.

The cardinal explained that there were twenty episcopal conferences in Africa which are grouped into nine regional conferences. The nine regional conferences make up a plenary assembly, with the cardinal as president. The plenary assembly, or Pan-African Secretariat, has two secretary bishops: Archbishop Jean

Baptiste Zoa, of Yaoundé, Cameroons, is French-language secretary; Bishop Joseph Blomjous, W.F., of Mwanza, Tanganyika, is English-language secretary. In addition, there are two secretary priests, the Reverend Stephen Wellens, W.F., who teaches at a major seminary in Kachebere, Nyasaland, and the Reverend Joseph Greco, S.J., who teaches at a regional seminary in Tananarive, Malagasy Republic. They are, respectively, English and French speaking.

The nine regional conferences, the cardinal continued, are based on geographical divisions of the bishops. Each regional conference designates a bishop to take part in each commission that the African Council Fathers have set up to parallel the Council's ten commissions and the Secretariat for Promoting Christian Unity. These eleven African commissions of bishops follow the work of the Council commissions in the name of the whole Pan-African Secretariat.

Each of the regional conferences has a president. These presidents may meet whenever necessary to discuss common problems to be presented to the Council. Thus, Dahomey-born Archbishop Bernardin Gantin, of Cotonou, presides over the bishops of French-speaking West Africa (including Mali, Upper Volta, Senegal, Guinea, Dahomey and Togo). Ghanaian Archbishop John K. Amissah, of Cape Coast, Ghana, presides over the conference for English-speaking West Africa (Ghana, Sierra Leone, Liberia). Bishop Anthony Nivedo, C.S.Sp., of Umuahia, Nigeria, speaks for the bishops of Nigeria. Archbishop Zoa, a native of Cameroons, presides over the conference that includes what was formerly French Central Africa—Cameroons, the Congo (Brazzaville), Gabon, Chad and the Central African Republic. South Africa-born Archbishop Owen McCann, of Cape Town, South Africa, heads the conference of South Africa and Southern Rhodesia. French-born Archbishop Léon-Etienne Duval, of Algiers, represents North Africa (Morocco, Algeria and Tunisia). English-speaking East Africa (Uganda, Kenya, Tanganyika, Northern Rhodesia, Nyasaland and Sudan) is represented by Dutch-born Bishop Blomjous. What was formerly

Belgian Central Africa—the Congo (Leopoldville), Rwanda and Burundi—is gathered in a conference of bishops presided over by Belgian-born Archbishop Félix Scalais, C.I.C.M., of Leopoldville. French-born Archbishop Jean Wolff, C.S.Sp., of Diégo-Suarez, Malagasy Republic, heads the conference that includes Malagasy Republic, Mozambique and Angola.

I knew that the cardinal had made special studies of the social and educational work in East Africa. His doctoral thesis in Rome had been on that subject. I asked him if he thought the Council might touch on these matters. He spoke first about education:

In all countries, education is of vital importance for the people. The Church in Africa is aware of this and has tried her very best, in cooperation with the governments, to establish schools at all levels, from elementary to university education. There are social centers, too, in many places, that are at the disposition of even old people who wish to gain some knowledge. In the Second Vatican Council's program there are whole chapters devoted to the magisterium of the Church, studies in the seminaries and universities, and even the communications media. All of this certainly shows the great concern of the Church in such matters.

The cardinal was counting on the Catholic schools of East Africa to produce leaders of the future, and he could already point to a number of leaders that had been trained in those schools. I knew that he had organized the National Union of St. Augustine to train leaders for public life. It was in connection with the topic of social work in the Church that the cardinal presented some deeper ideas about Christian leadership:

The popes have dealt with the topic of social work in many of their encyclical letters, discourses and talks to pilgrims visiting Rome. It is obvious that the Church will never keep aloof in matters concerning the development of people with a view to public life. Many of the leading figures in public life have been students at the Church's institutions. The mission of the Church is to train the whole man to be Christlike, to bring Christ into every walk of life. Christian leadership is needed in order to cope with the ever-advancing trends of modern life.

The cardinal then quoted, in Latin, something that Cardinal Agagianian had said (the translation is mine): "The Church holds that she has a specific contribution to make to the solution of human problems; it is to be seen in her preaching of the Gospel, which does not exclude the social problems that cause such serious anxiety to men of our times. In preaching the kingdom of God, which our Lord likened to yeast penetrating the whole mass around it (Matt. 13:33), and in spreading the law of charity throughout the world, the Church generates the dispositions which nourish social progress and develop into justice."

The cardinal referred at this point to several sentences in a joint pastoral letter that he and the bishops of Tanganyika had presented in December, 1960: "Social action, however, has its own aim: the betterment of human temporal order. . . . Social action prepares the human temporal milieu for the reception of the message of Christ. . . . Christians should be motivated by supernatural charity, love and compassion for their fellowmen in need. At the same time, we should hope and pray that these our human efforts for the temporal good of our fellowmen will be used by God for their spiritual benefit, in His own way and in His own time.

"Therefore," the cardinal continued, "social problems, inasmuch as they touch the very mission of the Church, will be treated accordingly in the Ecumenical Council."

The editors of *America* had presented large extracts from that pastoral letter in the documentation section of *The Catholic Mind* (January, 1962), and we had just presented an editorial, in the March 30, 1963, issue of *America*, which referred to the document as "a joint pastoral letter on Church and State that could well become the blueprint for the future relationship of the religious and the civil societies in the new Africa." As the bishops explained at the beginning of the letter, they set out "to explain the principles regarding the duty of all Catholics, both as individuals and as members of organized groups, to collaborate with the State and with all its citizens in the realization of the aim of human society, the common good of all citizens." The letter contains the authentic voice of the teaching Church in up-to-date language that confronts what people today would regard as "real" questions, e.g., "Faced as it is with existence in a pluralistic society, what directives can the Church give to its children living in a divided world?" The document was *aggiornamento* at its best, and all the more impressive coming from an African hierarchy whose spectacular growth is more than matched by the articulateness of its members—a striking phenomenon of the modern Church.

The cardinal reasserted a point made in the pastoral letter: "The welfare of human society and of a particular country—that is to say, the common good—largely depends on the widening of the basis of common agreement between individuals and varying groups, and on their common pursuit of basic beneficial goals. This cooperation is urged on us not only by our love of country but by our love of our neighbors and of God.

"It is evident," the cardinal continued, "from reflection on the basic principles of the equality and dignity of man, that the same human and civic rights must be guaranteed to each and every member of every nationality, race or tribe living in any country. All are equal as human beings—not according to capacity, of course, but according to dignity. All are creatures, and children, of God. All are rational and free, with the same origin, the same nature, the same supernatural destiny. The human race is one. Discrimination against any nationality, race or tribe would be clearly contrary to the natural law."

Yes, it was the authentic teaching voice of the Church, but coming from the Negro cardinal, head of the hierarchy of Africa, with the references to tribes added to what any other bishop of the Church would have said, it was especially striking. And so were the following words: "The natural law clearly endows groups who follow a certain type of intellectual or spiritual tradition with the right to continued existence in that tradition, whether they be in the majority or minority. They have a right to the acceptance and recognition of those values inherent in their traditions, so long as this is not clearly inconsistent with the common good of society."

Coming back to education and social action, the cardinal said:

"Social services—e.g., education, social security, medico-social insurance, community development and so forth—should not fall under the exclusive domain of the State. That, too, is evident from the principles of the natural law. Only a false concept of the State would lead us to believe that it has complete and absolute control over society or over the social field."

At an episcopal conference held recently at Dar-es-Salaam, in Tanganyika, Bishop Joseph Kilasara, of Moshi, had read a paper entitled "Church and State in the New Africa." Catholics may soon have their "backs to the wall," the bishop warned, unless they take steps now to cope with trends toward nationalism, socialism, naturalism and even totalitarianism. Bishop Kilasara, proposed that the Church consider scrapping the independent mission-school system in favor of a "unified governmental system of education," provided the State would continue to respect the ideological orientation of different schools. The bishop proposed a single unified service of hospitals, clinics and charitable organizations along the same lines. He was trying to avoid both the withering away of the mission school and the complete, absolute nationalization of all schools and social services.

The cardinal pointed out that in their joint pastoral letter the bishops of Tanganyika had admitted there must be some form of pluralism in the social field as a requisite safeguard against false doctrine about the State and against practical totalitarianism. They saw that social pluralism could take three possible forms: 1) integral social pluralism, a system of entirely private social services; 2) a social pluralism allowing for parallel systems of public and private social services; 3) a form or system in which all private services are integrated in one public service. In theory, any of these systems would be unobjectionable in the light of the natural law, "so long as it would really provide the social services required by the common good while guaranteeing the rights of the family and of different ideological groups, and the freedom of the human person." The cardinal said that integral social pluralism, the first of the three possibilities, "hardly seems feasible in the world of today, a world in which the State has to play an increasing role in the social field." In these days of advanced organization and development, "more complex systems have to be worked out in practice; they must include state subsidies for social activities of nongovernmental agencies." The rights of the State over social institutions "do extend to the effective right of organizing and integrating the different social services. In fact, subsidization of voluntary agencies is an indispensable condition for the assurance of the continued existence of social pluralism.

"The state," the cardinal continued, "is not the same thing as society. It is, rather, the public order as a living action in society. That action is directed at a limited and external end, which is the happiness of man in the temporal order. The State has the role of supervising and integrating all activities in the social field. In a pluralistic society, Catholics can and should collaborate with all other citizens in the political and social field.

"The State has the right to organize this collaboration," he added, "as long as it remains in the temporal order. On the other hand, the Church has the right and duty of directing this collaboration on the part of her faithful, in order that there be no detriment to their religious life. The State is a real power, ordained by God as such, but its power is over human things, for the fostering of the common good of society. The State has no rights over the religious convictions of its citizens, but it does have the duty of fostering religion. It must in a real way acknowledge God in its work; it must recognize the belief of its citizens in God; it must recognize their acceptance of the order of natural law.

"Furthermore," the cardinal stressed, "the State must guarantee freedom of religion. The State cannot force any citizen to practice a religion that is repugnant to his conscience. The state must be completely impartial about beliefs and religions. Therefore, no public servant has any right to show himself biased in favor of his coreligionists in carrying out his duties. We believe, of course, that the Catholic Church is the one true Church, but we firmly believe also that the State will best help the Catholic Church by not forcing the conscience of any citizen and by guaranteeing freedom of religion. In pursuing the common good, we believe the State will, in effect, create the temporal milieu that is most favorable to the workings of God's grace and most favorable to a sincere, free, truly human search for the truth.

"We can put it this way," the cardinal said: "As Catholics, convinced of having the complete religious truth, we have the duty of helping all others to share this truth and to live according to it. All of us have this duty. We must live in close contact with the people around us. We cannot retire to an inner circle of Catholics living in isolation from the rest of the world. We must have the dynamic love of neighbor which takes us to every place where we can serve. By living in the midst of our fellowmen and showing practical interest in their welfare, we can become in some measure the 'salt of the earth' and the 'light of the world.' To accomplish this, we must respect the freedom of conscience of our neighbors and the essential freedom of the act of faith. We should accept and respect everything that is good and true in other religions. Yes, there is truth outside the Catholic Church. There is some truth in all religions, and we must venerate truth wherever we find it, for it can have come from only one source, from God."

In their joint pastoral letter, the bishops of Tanganyika had stressed "using spiritual means to reach our spiritual goal." In their view, "politics, political instruments or political power are not means of religious proselytism . . . nor are social action—education, medical facilities, social services, etc." The cardinal pointed to what followed in the letter: "The apostolate of the laity is a participation of the laity in the apostolate of the hierarchy of the Church. It is an apostolate in the strict sense. It has to do with the spiritual level, or with the temporal order inasmuch as it is directly touched by the spiritual. It is the apostolate of the layman in the very pastoral work of the Church itself, spreading the kingdom of God." The social action of Catholics, the cardinal pointed out, prolongs the influence of the Church into the social and political field, but it is distinct from the direct apostolate of the laity. "Nevertheless," he added, "although these two types of action by Catholics are distinct, they are not separate. In fact, there is an inseparable relation between them. We may put it this way: the lay apostolate leads to social action and prepares one for it, because even on the temporal level our actions must proceed from Christian inspiration—from God."

Toward the end of the pastoral letter, there was this sentence: "Besides this direct apostolate, we must be ever mindful of the value of the indirect apostolate which allows our fellowmen to live in their own religions in such a way as to enable them more and more to respond to the interior appeal of God's grace." The cardinal drew my attention to an earlier passage in the letter: "To make our position quite clear and to avoid misunderstanding, we again proclaim, and firmly, that we Catholics do not doubt the possibility, nor deny the fact, of the sincerity of the majority of non-Catholics. . . . They are following their conscience. . . . Every human being is born with the indestructible right of following his conscience. This right will apply to every field, especially to the religious field."

This clear, frank presentation by the cardinal and the bishops of Tanganyika was typical of what the Fathers of the Second Vatican Council had heard whenever the spokesman for the bishops of Africa rose to speak. With quiet dignity and awareness of realities, the fruit of experience, Cardinal Rugambwa, I knew, had communicated strength and encouragement to those whose work and ideas he endorsed. It was so because he spoke not only with awareness of the power of the Church in Africa, but also because he spoke with awareness of the power of God. He said, in conclusion: "You understand that a lot of points are under consideration, so we cannot know what will be decided until after the Council. Still, we hope very great things will be done by the Council for the greater glory of God and the salvation of souls." His trust in the power of God will certainly continue to be a source of strength and encouragement.

VIII

THE CHURCH,

BISHOPS AND THE BIBLE

Bernard Cardinal Alfrink, Archbishop of Utrecht and a president of the Second Vatican Council, earned his doctorate in biblical studies in 1930 from the Pontifical Biblical Commission in Rome. During the next fifteen years he became one of the most highly regarded Catholic biblical scholars in Europe. Whatever he would say about the Bible, I knew, would be especially important. Whatever he would say about the life of the Church in a modern pluralistic society would also be listened to with great respect because, as head of the hierarchy of Holland, he speaks from years of experience in a country whose religious makeup has been the object of special study throughout the world in a Church-State context. The cardinal spoke out quite frankly on these topics but also with obviously great care and precision.

The future cardinal was born on July 5, 1900, at Nijkerk, in the central Netherlands, a predominantly Protestant little town. He was one of seven children. The father of the family was a contractor. In 1913, young Bernard Jan Alfrink entered the minor seminary at Culemborg. In 1919, he moved up to the major seminary at Driebergen. On August 15, 1924, he was ordained to the priesthood. After ordination, he was sent to study at the Pontifical Biblical Institute. After receiving the doctorate, he returned to Holland and spent three years in parish work at Houten and Maarssen. He was then named professor of Sacred Scripture at the archdiocesan seminary in Rijsenburg.

By 1944, Father Alfrink was such a well-established scholar that he was appointed a consultor to the Pontifical Commission of Biblical Studies. The following year, he became professor of biblical exegesis at the Catholic University of Nijmegen. For the most part, he taught courses in Old Testament and Hebrew. Together with Professor G. C. Hartman, he prepared the "Pericopes" translation of the Epistles and Gospels, for the readings during Mass in the Netherlands. It is the text that is still used at Mass. In the Dutch translation of the Bible that was made in those years, called the "Petrus Canisius" translation, the future cardinal contributed the books of Ecclesiastes, Ecclesiasticus, Wisdom and Tobias.

On May 28, 1951, Pope Pius XII named him Coadjutor Archbishop of Utrecht. John Cardinal de Jong, Archbishop of Utrecht, had retired to a convent because of poor health. When Cardinal de Jong died, in September, 1955, Archbishop Alfrink was named administrator of the archdiocese. On November 4, 1955, Pope Pius named him Archbishop of Utrecht and head of the metropolitan province that includes all of the Netherlands (besides Utrecht, the dioceses of Breda, Haarlem, Roermond, Groningen, Rotterdam and 's Hertogenbosch). In August, 1957, he became the first military vicar of the Dutch armed forces. Pope John proclaimed Archbishop Alfrink a cardinal in the consistory of March 28, 1960. Three months later, he was named a member of the Central Preparatory Commission of the Second Vatican Council.

When I met the cardinal at his house in Utrecht, I noticed how much he resembles Cardinal Cushing. I knew that, like Cardinal Cushing, he had a wide range of interests. He had for years encouraged a wide, international outlook in the Catholic press of Holland. He had been probing the whole question of new roles for the laity, the field of Catholic-Protestant relationships, the whole subject of youth guidance. In his first pastoral letter as Archbishop of Utrecht he had presented a survey of religious conditions in Holland and had made the flat statement that "there is no greater enemy of the Church than Catholics who disgrace their faith."

In 1952, at the opening of a Catholic hospital in Hengelo, the cardinal said, with typical frankness and outspokenness, that care of the sick should not be an exclusive task of the State but that Church and State should cooperate in providing medical aid. At a national meeting in Hilversum, in 1958, the cardinal stated it was an affront to human dignity that families should have to live in overcrowded quarters. He said: "There are not enough houses being built today for bigger families." He insisted that parents who wanted to have large families should be given the opportunity of doing so.

In 1961, at a seminar in Strasbourg, France, Cardinal Alfrink said that "the Catholic Church should sacrifice nonessential elements of her life that tend to confuse non-Catholics about the true nature of her unity. While unity of faith is essential and indivisible, the ways in which the faith can be practiced are variable." It was in this spirit that the cardinal answered my questions.

QUESTION

In Your Eminence's overall view of the Council to date, what seem to be the Council's achievements?

CARDINAL ALFRINK

If one attempts to discern what the Second Vatican Council will produce in concrete details, it must be admitted there is very little that one can predict with certainty at the moment. However, one thing certainly became evident during the first session of the Council. It is a matter that must be seen to have the greatest importance for the further development of the Council. It is something that practically cannot be undone. I refer to the fact that the Council—that is to say, the Church —has declared for a definite course, and by an unexpectedly great majority. That is the great gain of the period marked by this first session of the Council.

One could meet bishops in Rome who were not enthusiastic about what happened at the Council. They did not find that first session very efficient. After two months of deliberations, they felt, there was so little that one could bring back home in the way of concrete results. They forgot two things.

Those bishops forgot, first, how this first session emphasized before the whole Church and before the whole world with what freedom the bishops could express the ideas by which they thought they could serve the Church. It was quite evident that they were not called to Rome merely to listen. It was evident that they were there, first of all, as shepherds of the Church together with the Pope; they were there to pass judgment and to speak. From that one fact—that there was common deliberation by the Pope and the bishops of the world —the value and significance of a council are discerned. The Roman Curia as such, however serviceable and necessary it may be in the normal administration of the Church, has no task, no function, at a council except to render pure service. That task, that function, however, can be quite important if it is fulfilled in the proper spirit. If a council is going to function properly, the freedom of the bishops must be guaranteed. In the first session of the Council, that freedom was fully acknowledged.

In the second place, the bishops who were not enthusiastic about the first session forgot how significant and how important it was that the Council should have declared for a definite course during that first session. Now, as I say, whatever the desires of Council Fathers may have been, the period of that first session took a definite course. There have been many descriptions of that first session as a period of tuning in, but I believe it was more. It was a period of getting to know the terrain, yes, but it was even more than that. Not only did we learn the terrain; the path was determined on which the Council would proceed further. The bishops declared themselves clearly on this matter, and the Holy Father sanctioned the path that was determined. The Holy Father sanctioned it with a clarity which, in the given circumstances, could not be more definite. It is quite evident, and it is quite natural, that every opinion and every group tries to claim the Holy Father as a supporter, but here is the fact in this case: the Holy Father announced himself very plainly about the general tendency according to which the Council should go, without this direction in all its details being determined. Thus, one can say, the character of this Second Vatican Council is determined, and future sessions cannot do much to alter it.

The direction which the Council chose has been described in various fashions. Each adjective used for the purpose indicates one or another aspect. Ordinarily, one speaks in this connection of "pastoral" and "ecumenical." The direction of the Council is called "open." It is open with respect to the Church's internal affairs, insofar as within the Church it leaves open more possibilities; there is the possibility of more diversity and less uniformity, in the spirit of the council of the Apostles (Acts 15), which prescribes only what is most necessary and leaves other matters free. The direction chosen by the Council is open insofar as it looks less to juridical precision and allows for more spontaneity and charismatic expansion. It is open, also, insofar as it makes communication more convenient between the central point of the Church and the local hierarchy, between hierarchy and faithful. It is open also with respect to the exterior, insofar as the Council is directed, not only to the Church itself but also, and perhaps first of all, or at least permanently, to the world outside the Church. The Council—the Church—is aware that it has the task of preaching salvation to all mankind, and not only of caring for the salvation of those who already believe in her.

Thus, on reflection, one sees that the Council should speak in a way that differs from the manner adopted by previous Councils. In this twentieth century, the world has grown smaller. As a result of developments in technology and the communications media, the whole of mankind has come to have a sense of community. Now, for the first time, all humanity can be reached by the Church with the message of salvation. These facts require that the Church speak at this time with a language that all humanity can understand. When the Church intends to speak to all humanity and has the chance to reach all humanity effectively with every word, when by and through the Council she asks and draws the attention of all mankind, she cannot be satisfied to speak in scholastic formulae.

Of course, these scholastic formulae are also necessary in God's Church, but, one reflects, the Church must do more. She must present to humanity the evangelical message of salvation that Christ brought to the world and that the Church continues on earth. The Council must present that message to mankind in a manner which people today, believers or unbelievers, can understand, just as the Lord did in the Gospels— open and warm, attentive to the needs and the longings of mankind today. This is to be done, of course, without diminishing the Gospel of salvation at all. It is to be done by inviting attractively, by encouraging and consoling according to the word of the Lord: "Come to me, all ye who labor and are burdened, and I will give you rest." In accordance with this tendency, the Council will be more apt to speak in a biblical, evangelical fashion rather than in a scholastic tone.

Every council in the history of the Church has spoken in a manner required by the times. It makes very little sense, therefore, to point to earlier Councils which once upon a time spoke thus and so. Each Council, when it spoke, used a language that corresponded to the requirements of the times. The Second Vatican Council must realize that it speaks to the world of today, which is quite different from that of the Council of Trent, or even of the First Vatican Council.

Should this Second Vatican Council pay no attention, then, to the dangers of errors and misconceptions which arise within the Church perhaps precisely by this open approach to all the world and by contact with all the systems of thought and the various human opinions with which Christians of today are confronted? Of course, the Council must do that, but, one can see on reflection, it should not only do that.

There cannot be any bishop in the Church who does not have the intention of presenting clearly, in its purity, the teaching which the Church must preach. In this respect, all of the various currents of opinion which appeared in the Council are fundamentally one. It is not necessary that everything which is at present under discussion in the Church should be brought up and settled by the Council. What is clearly in contradiction with the unchanging teaching of the Church, that the Church must reject. But she should do this as a mother, more in the spirit of instructing than of judging—if it is possible, more encouraging than repulsing. Although there are theories or concepts which the Church must reject—especially as they concern people outside the Church who do not possess the full light or complete truth—there are also respectable and worthy elements present. So the Church should be open to them. She should value what is really of value; she should point out, by her instruction, what is erroneous and misguided.

Discussion between the two tendencies which manifested themselves at the Council does not concern evangelical truth as such. No one wants to depart from that. The discussion concerns the presentation of truth to the world today. The discussion is not about the nature of the Church but about the human arrangement of the Church. Each bishop loves the Church with all his heart and wishes the Church could be seen by all humanity, so that it would be captivated by the Church. Also, discussion does not touch on the rights of the Church but on the question whether the Church shall lay the principal emphasis on these rights rather than on the task which she has received from God, to bring all mankind "into the kingdom of his beloved Son, in whom we have our redemption, the remission of our sins" (Col. 1:13-14).

QUESTION

Our American bishops, in a pastoral letter, said they were going to the Council not "empty-handed" but with a store of experience gained from the existence of the Church in the pluralistic society of the United States. Could Your Eminence comment on the feelings of a Dutch prelate going to the Council with the experiences of the Church in the Netherlands?

CARDINAL ALFRINK

Perhaps it is because of their experiences that the bishops who come from countries with a religiously mixed population are more sensitive on this point than bishops from homogeneously Catholic countries. Every day they are confronted with the problem which is the consequence of dwelling together as one people. The relation of Church and State in the practical order as they know it is quite different from the way it is in so-called Catholic countries, quite apart from the question whether there are still any Catholic countries in the world.

In countries with a religiously pluralistic population the Church must collaborate in devising a practical arrangement for harmonious dwelling together. She cannot be closed on herself, and she must not think only of herself. She must look out beyond her boundaries; she must reckon with those who do not belong to her as children; and she must announce the message of salvation to all. The message of the Church must be announced without impairing the truth. But if the Church wants to be heard she shall—with proper regard for special cases—not speak polemically but irenically; she should not repel but draw by her insistence. The Church can never approve the perverse things that she meets with, but she can recognize and value the good wherever she meets it. In pluralistic countries, the Church should be ready to work with all others who welcome such an open approach.

Holland is perhaps an example of a pluralistic country. Speaking in round numbers, about 40 percent of the population is Catholic, about 40 percent is Protestant, and about 20 percent belongs to no religious body. Holland is also an example of democratic freedom; the State recognizes the same rights for all citizens. On the basis of this principle, the

Church in our country enjoys a great measure of freedom and a certain support from the State, such as in many a so-called Catholic country is unknown. The most significant example of this is the Dutch legislation on education.

Although the rights of the Church are perhaps better pre-served in Holland than in many another country, we prefer to speak of the rights of the Catholic citizen, who does not ask for a privileged position but only for the same rights and freedom as his fellow citizens. As a consequence, the Catholic citizen is ready to give the same rights and freedoms to his fellow citizens insofar as this is not in conflict with the law of the land. In this understanding of the matter, there is no recognition for error or unbelief—can such beliefs be a sub-ject, a bearer of rights?—but the possibility of living is given to people who are in error or who do not believe. The Church cannot intend to take it away from them.

It is this common living in one land and one people, as citizens with equal rights, which gives bishops from such countries perhaps a greater facility in grasping the "openness" of the Church. But it is by no means true that only bishops from these countries have such a grasp. This is something that by now has become quite evident at the Council.

QUESTION

The pastoral letter of Your Eminence and the other Dutch bishops on the Second Vatican Council has been reprinted and studied in many countries around the world. Could you com-ment on that pastoral letter in the light of experiences at the Council?

CARDINAL ALFRINK

If you mean to inquire whether the Dutch bishops during the Council learned that many bishops all over the world had read their pastoral letter, then I can give a specific answer of a more positive nature. Moreover, I can add that very many bishops, according to what they say, found themselves in full agreement with it when they read it.

As you know, this pastoral letter was intended to serve as a preparation for the Council. It speaks, therefore, about the Council, that is to say, about the bishops who were summoned to a general assembly by the Pope in order to deliberate together with him about the Church. This exceptional event of a Council seemed to the bishops a sufficient reason to speak about the task and function and position of the college of bishops in the Church—obviously, only with the Pope and not without the Pope, as was stated in numberless pages of the pastoral letter.

It is, in fact, very probable that the Second Vatican Council will not neglect to draw special attention to the function of the world episcopacy, the bishops' college in the Church. The First Vatican Council also did that, though on account of the sudden adjournment of the Council, nothing of a complete nature was pronounced. Nevertheless, in the *acta* of this First Vatican Council, you can find the foundation for a further defining and treatment of the episcopal function. It is, therefore, also self-evident why so many publications on this question saw the light in this time of the Second Vatican Council.

In all sincerity it should be said that no one has the idea of attacking the position of the papacy in the Church. This was clearly defined in the First Vatican Council, and every believing and faithful Catholic accepts it from his heart.

As you know, however, there are many bishops who ask, in this matter of the Church, if the college of bishops could not be more entrusted with the government of the Church than is now the case. They also believe that it could be useful to have more communication, more discussion and cooperation between the Curia and the local hierarchy—again, I say, in the interests of the Church. They think that the management of affairs which at present is carried on mostly by the Roman Curia and papal representatives in the different countries could function more conveniently and better if the local hierarchy were entrusted with more of it. These bishops are of the opinion that this would not endanger any dogmas of the Church, and that it is only a matter of serving the interests of the Church.

QUESTION

Interest in the Bible is on the increase everywhere. Other countries could learn much from developments in this field in the Netherlands. I am thinking of the Bible retreats, programs of Bible distribution and other interesting developments in your country. Would Your Eminence say something about the biblical movement and the modern world?

CARDINAL ALFRINK

The biblical movement and the ecumenical movement are undoubtedly two expressions of the life of the Church which are very closely related. It is difficult to say which is more important.

The development of the art of printing completely changed the reading situation at the end of the fifteenth century and the beginning of the sixteenth. Before that, a book—which was copied by hand—was a costly item that only a few men could permit themselves. Moreover, and also on account of this, only a few people could read. The knowledge of the faith for the mass of the people was based upon preaching and the "poor man's Bible" of paintings, carvings and windows in cathedrals and village churches.

As the art of printing spread, the Bible became one of the first books to be printed, in part or in entirety. This was already decades before Luther nailed his theses on the door of the castle chapel of Wittenberg (supposing that this story is still to be taken as a historical occurrence). In proportion as the printed complete text of the Bible came within the reach of everybody, to that extent the problem was increased, due to the fact that the Church's preparation was not quite complete. It was not always easy for every reader to see how the preaching of the Church after a development of fifteen centuries was still ultimately the same as the teaching of Holy Scripture. We cannot deny that the general distribution of the Scriptures among people who were not sufficiently prepared to read them offered great opportunities for the Reformation.

It is easy to understand, therefore, that the Counter Reformation exercised a certain degree of caution with respect to the spread and general reading of Scripture. They settled on the formula which in itself is quite fair: "The reading of Scripture is useful but not necessary." The preaching of the Church, by which the written word of God comes to us, is sufficient in order to know the truth which the Lord has brought us. They spoke also of the two tables which Holy Mother Church sets for her children and by which she offers us the word of God. One is the table of the Eucharist, at which the Church breaks the bread of life for her children. The other is the table of the liturgy, in which the Church breaks the other bread of life, the written word of God, and offers her faithful the pericopes and other sections of the Bible which she has chosen. You find this idea, for instance, in the *Imitation of Christ,* and it is also elaborated in the book by the Vicar Apostolic of the mission of Holland, Johannes van Neercassel, who used to reside in Utrecht. His book, published in the seventeenth century, was about the reading of Holy Scripture.

In recent decades—but well before the ecumenical movement began to develop—the development of Catholic biblical knowledge and perhaps a new theological view of the value of Holy Scripture in the totality of the Church's preaching brought into prominence the idea that the written word of God should assume a more fundamental position in Catholic spirituality. Why shouldn't the faithful have personal knowledge of the salvation history of the Old and New Testaments? God's Spirit Himself has described that history in the books of Scripture. Has God given Holy Scripture to His Church in order that it should be read only in parts and by certain people? Or can it be a precious source of spirituality for the faithful as they learn to know God just as He has revealed Himself in Holy Scripture; as their piety is nourished and strengthened with the great—and the grand—thoughts which are found in Scripture; as they learn to praise, adore and thank God with the words inspired by God's Spirit; as they are urged on by God's own words to serve God as His gracious concern speaks to us in Scripture?

Holy Scripture is not only a source of revelation; it is also a source of spiritual life. In the course of centuries, an immeasurable stream of excellent literature has flowed forth in the Church with the aim of nourishing the spiritual life of the faithful. But why should we put the word of God itself on the second plane? Because it is not always easy to understand? Because it can give rise to misunderstanding and perverted interpretation? These considerations that have just been mentioned make all the plainer that it is not sufficient merely to distribute a great quantity of Bibles. One should also teach the faithful how to read the Holy Scriptures, and one should also serve as a companion to them in their reading of the Holy Scripture. Hence the many little Bible clubs which originate in our parishes, where people read the Scripture together under the direction of a priest, and the Scripture is explained as a source of nourishment for the spiritual life of the people. The same thing happens at the so-called Bible retreats, where the great thoughts of Scripture, which wholly dominate human life and the life of believing Christians, are illuminated by the word of God. Those thoughts are looked for in the Scripture itself, and they are presented in a scriptural terminology. They get acquainted with the Scripture, and so people learn to understand scriptural language.

In the matter of biblical distribution, there is a notable cooperation between the Catholic Bible Society of St. Willibrord, established some years ago (and named after the first preacher of the faith in this region, the first Bishop of

Utrecht), and the already longer existing Protestant association, the Netherlands Bible Society, which has very great experience in this field. The Protestant Bible society has also given especially valuable help, with great willingness, in the publishing of a new translation of the New Testament. It was published in 1961 by a group of Catholic Bible scholars.

In many places, the two organizations—the Catholic Bible foundation and the Protestant Bible society—have developed joint activities for the spread of Holy Scripture. The Catholic version of the Bible is placed in Catholic families, the Protestant version in non-Catholic families. Together they go out to sell Bibles at every door. This common action may appear to be somewhat remarkable, but it manifests a worthily ecumenical aspect. It demonstrates how Catholic and Protestant Christians, in spite of all differences in their concept of faith, have actually a common basis, that is to say, belief in our Lord Jesus Christ, whose message is announced in Scripture. Consciousness of this unity—even imperfect, as it is—is a first opening of doors and a pressure for getting rid of further barriers. This going together—each with his own Bible—demonstrates the separation which exists and which the Lord has not intended, and it thus awakens desire for a greater unity, for the complete unity the Lord has willed.

I understand that in your own mind you have the question if it is not possible that Protestants and Catholics could possess and use one and the same Bible text. However much this also is to be desired, and however great the longing for it is among very many, a project like that has first of all to overcome considerable difficulties.

These difficulties probably lie not so much in the ecclesiastical regulations that translations of Scripture for Catholics must be provided with footnotes (Canon 1391). This shows merely that for Catholics their own editions are necessary in spite of the fact that Catholic and Protestant translators work from the same texts of Scripture. More difficulty is created by the fact that in the course of centuries Catholics and Protestants have developed peculiar idioms for certain biblical concepts. The faithful in each case have become so accustomed to these idioms that they can hardly understand another terminology.

This is the case at least in the language of the Netherlands, where Protestants and Catholics have their own expressions for certain biblical concepts. I assume that the same would also be true in countries of other languages. I find here no solution except that one group should sacrifice its own idiom and make use of the other's idiom. A compromise is not possible. I am not talking here about the spelling of proper names, whether they follow the Hebrew spelling or that of the Vulgate. Such a difficulty is not insoluble. But I am thinking, for instance, of a concept such as "temptation," which is given, in Dutch, as *verzoeking* for Protestants and *bekoring* for Catholics. Each group scarcely understands the favored terminology of the other. In this way, too, it also happens that translations practically always contain a certain amount of interpretation, especially where texts indicate a difference of exegetical understanding or even of different theological visions. Some ten years ago, some of the Protestant church societies which had very strong theological differences undertook to work out a translation of the Bible together. Those who were on the inside of that project know what great difficulties they met with, especially in the theologically pregnant texts. They finally came to grips with the problem, but often they could find the solution only in compromise, which was not always satisfactory for everyone.

It is quite evident, therefore, that very many difficulties have to be overcome before we can have a common translation of Holy Scripture. But this fact does not impair the thought that a uniform translation of the Bible to be used by Protestants and Catholics is of great value from an ecumenical point of view.

When I was leaving the cardinal's house that night, he accompanied me to the door. On the way, we passed a mantelpiece on which stood one framed photograph. It was a photostatic copy of a page from the records of the Italian army. The entire page concerned a soldier named Roncalli. With a twinkle in his eyes, the cardinal drew my attention to the description of the soldier—color of eyes, hair, etc. The cardinal took great delight in the description of the soldier's character. It was a good record. The cardinal had received his copy from the Italian Minister of Defense, who had given a dinner during the first session of the Second Vatican Council for the Council Fathers who were military vicars. We talked for several minutes more about the soldier who had become Pope John XXIII. When the full story of the Second Vatican Council is told, I believe it will be seen that few, if any, of the Council Fathers esteemed Pope John XXIII more highly than Cardinal Alfrink.

IX

FORWARD-LOOKING

OPENNESS

The Most Reverend Ermenegildo Florit, Archbishop of Florence, Italy, received me in a room of his great house that has a view of the famous domed baptistry and, beyond, the towering Cathedral of Florence. Readers of the Catholic press, if asked to identify the Archbishop of Florence, would probably refer to him as the bishop who called a meeting of his laity before the first session of the Second Vatican Council, in order, as he put it, to have full knowledge of his people's desires. He told me that he planned to hold a similar meeting before the second session of the Council, and that most likely he would continue to call other meetings of the laity after the close of the Council. He told me he thought such meetings might well become an institution in the Archdiocese of Florence.

This active interest in the lay apostolate was not something entirely new for the archbishop. He had been in charge of the women's division of Catholic Action, in Rome, some years before. But this had not been the main interest of his life. This remarkable, ruddy-faced, heavyset man in his sixties had been a professor of Sacred Scripture for a quarter of a century at the Pontifical Lateran University. He was born at Fagagna, in the Archdiocese of Udine, on July 5, 1901, and was ordained to the priesthood on April 11, 1925, after theological studies at the Lateran. He received the degree of Doctor of Sacred Scripture

[100]

after studies at the Pontifical Biblical Institute, and authored books on biblical inspiration and form criticism. He became a consultor of the Pontifical Commission of Biblical Studies. On July 12, 1954, he was named Coadjutor Archbishop of Florence, and he was consecrated on September 12. When Elia Cardinal Dalla Costa, Archbishop of Florence, died, December 21, 1961, Archbishop Florit became administrator of the archdiocese. He succeeded to the see on March 19, 1962.

In the course of our conversation, we came back several times to that famous meeting with the laity on June 23, 1962. The archbishop described the process of communication between people and bishop as "an ongoing one." He said: "The people have a right to speak to their bishop, for he is their father." At the end of that meeting on June 23, the archbishop told his people that he foresaw there would have to be changes in the catechism in order to set forth the basic theology of the Church regarding the role of the laity, in language that would meet the expectations of the people. Thus, he told them—and repeated it to me—one of the first answers in the catechism (to the question: Why did God make us?) would have to be, instead of "God made us to know Him, to love Him and to serve Him," something like: "God made us to know Him and to share in making Him known, to love Him and to share in making Him loved, to serve Him and to share in bringing others to His service."

The archbishop stressed, in talking with me, that the Fathers of the Council are very much aware that the Church exists to serve, and that in this function both priests and people share. This, he added, was already evident in the liturgical decrees approved by the Council Fathers at their first session.

It was in this spirit of sharing the work of the Church that Archbishop Florit called upon the various classes in his ancient see to join him in what was probably the most remarkable Chair of Unity Octave the people of Florence had ever seen. The archbishop described for me how he brought together a distinguished array of Council Fathers to preach on the intentions of the octave, from January 18 to 25. He made the arrangements, he said, in a spirit of "forward-looking openness, which is characteristic of the Second Vatican Council." From his desk he took a printed sheet that listed the names: Giacomo Cardinal Lercaro, Archbishop of Bologna; Archbishop Pericle Felici, Secretary General of the Second Vatican Council; African-born Auxiliary Bishop Cesare Gatimo, of Nyeri, Kenya; Russian-born Bishop Andrei Katkoff, of the Byzantine Rite; Bishop Jean Rupp, of Monaco; Bishop Emilio Guano, of Livorno; Auxiliary Bishop Enrico Bartoletti, of Lucca; Auxiliary Bishop Antonio Angioni, of Pisa.

"Obviously," said the archbishop, "this Chair of Unity Octave, with bishops preaching each night, is a result of my getting to know my brother bishops better at the Vatican Council."

From his desk he took two long sheets of paper on which he had typed something. At the top of the first page, in his own hand, he had put: *"Il mondo va alla Chiesa."* It was a statement he had composed as an announcement of the unusual Unity Octave. It began with that title ("The world goes to the Church," literally) and continued: "in truth, as never before, the whole world looks today to the Church and the Pope who has brought together in council an episcopate that is now present in all the regions of the earth and which represents all the races of mankind." The text continued with St. Paul's famous sentence: "There is neither Jew nor Greek . . ." (Gal. 3:28). In all the documents he would show me that afternoon—pastoral letters, addresses to his clergy, etc.—I noticed a rich use of Scripture. This statement continued with an optimistic picture of what the Second Vatican Council's "internal renovation of the Church" and "openness to dialogue with separated Christians" could achieve for Christian unity. The archbishop drew attention particularly to the fact that the Church included in her embrace peoples that were free and peoples that lived under ideological and political totalitarianism. A further reference to workers and other classes in the Church brought us back to that meeting with the laity.

The archbishop said he was impressed by the wide variety of

interests shown by his people that day, and so was I when he gave me a transcript of that meeting. He said about four hundred of the laity responded to his invitation to meet him in the large hall of the major seminary. The next meeting, he thought, might attract more, and he planned to use the larger hall in the Palazzo Pucci, which, he explained, was Vatican property leased to his archdiocese.

After an introductory statement by Monsignor Giuliano Agresti, the archbishop's delegate for the organization of the apostolate of the laity in Florence, a layman rose to speak. He said: "Your Excellency, it is a joy for me to speak with my bishop. It is the first time in my life that I have had such an opportunity." He wanted to talk about the fourth point in a list of twelve that had been drawn up as an agenda for this meeting. He wanted to talk about the idea that the Council was infallible and yet that we had to pray for it. He was soon moving through deep theology.

There were professors and professional people in the audience. There was a wide knowledge of history, the arts, education and labor conditions. Some rose to ask for better preparation for marriage. One asked that the Council not deal with Marxism lest it be thought political instead of religious. Another pleaded for one rate of charge in the Church's arrangements for marriages and funerals. Another gave a remarkable lecture on the liturgy, calling for restoration of the liturgical year in all its integrity. Some told the archbishop stories to illustrate or prove their points. One man wanted to know what there was for workers in the Council's plans. I gathered he was afraid the Council would not come up with anything good for them because there was too much class consciousness in the Church. "I speak in the name of my parish," said another, and it was about the liturgy that he wanted to speak. One man rose to apologize that he was going to talk about something that was not on the agenda. Another said: "Today I read a statement by Cardinal Léger: 'We need dialogue in the Church today between clergy and laity no less than we need obedience.' "

There was great interest at that meeting in the missionary

aspect of the Church. There was discussion about how racism in the United States, and conditions in Algeria, Latin America and elsewhere affected the image of the Church. The role of the laity was probably—no, in fact, certainly—the dominant theme of the four-hour meeting. In a story that I wrote for Religious News Service, describing the archbishop's recollections of the meeting, I said the archbishop was impressed by the wide variety of interests shown by his people when he listened to them for four hours in the large hall of the major seminary. The editor in New York thought I must have erred, that the archbishop must have talked to them for four hours, and he changed the sentence accordingly. The fact is, however, that the learned biblical scholar and archbishop sat there for four hours listening to his people.

"It was a sort of paraliturgical event, as one of my people pointed out," he said, "but it was nonetheless a true Christian community with its pastor." A few of his people, the archbishop added, seemed drawn toward the idea of *monoclassismo* (a class-less society), and he felt it necessary to explain the Church's social teaching on the matter. "In the very nature of things," he said, "there are different classes of society. Just as our Lord dealt with men of different classes, so must the Church, in the person of the bishop and the priests." He said, too, that he was encouraged by what he regarded as a "common and sensible feeling among the Italian people" that "the idea of worker-priests would not be acceptable in Italy." The people were right, he said, "in asking for chaplains to be assigned to groups of workers, but the chaplains' full-time work would be the priestly ministry."

The archbishop smiled as he recalled how "everybody spoke freely—as a father would want his children to do." Not absolutely everything that was said by them that afternoon, he admitted, was in perfect conformity with the principles of the faith, "but most of it was, and all of it came from the heart." At the end of the four hours, the archbishop spoke to the people and commented on a number of the points they had raised. He told them there would be a single rate of charge, or stipend, for marriage and funeral arrangements, but he reminded them that such matters were too particular for the Vatican Council to handle. He assured them that local problems of that nature would be handled by national conferences, which would be strengthened "immensely" by decree of the Council.

The archbishop had also asked his priests for their ideas before he went to the first session of the Council. He was very much impressed by their response, too. He had asked that they write to him about their desires and their points of view on matters that could or should come up at the Council. The replies, he said, gave him "a first orientation toward the *aggiornamento* that would have to come in diocesan legislation after the Council." With a large gesture indicating the bulk of the replies he had received, he said he had the basis of preparations already for a postconciliar synod. He told his priests, in a talk shortly before he left Florence to attend the first session of the Council, that the care of souls required revision of the parish structure, the vicariates and the very life of the clergy in Florence.

The biblical scholar was obviously a very busy pastor now. It seemed to me, as I met others in the city after my visit with the archbishop, that priests and people were taking it for granted that Archbishop Florit would be made a cardinal at the next consistory. Several people told me that Florence was being represented at an Ecumenical Council for the first time by an archbishop who was not a cardinal. They expected that this anomaly would be set right before the next session of the Council. I smiled at their impatience. After all, the archbishop had headed the see only a few months when the Council began. But it was more than a point of historical honor with them, I discerned. It was obvious that their archbishop had won them with his attention to the apostolate of the laity, and they wanted him to have the highest privileges that anyone could have.

X

FULLER DISCOVERY

OF CHRIST

The Most Reverend Gerald Emmett Carter, D.D., Auxiliary
Bishop of London in the Province of Ontario, Canada, was born
of Irish-Canadian parents on March 1, 1912, in Montreal. His
mother was born in New York, of Irish immigrant parents, and
his father was a fourth-generation Canadian of Irish descent. The
future bishop went to St. Patrick's Elementary School in Montreal, and then to Montreal College, a French classical school
run by the Sulpician Fathers. By the time he entered the Grand
Seminary of Montreal, he had an excellent command of French
as well as English. He was ordained to the priesthood on March
22, 1937.

With a degree in theology already behind him, Father Carter
went on to earn a master's degree and a doctorate in the
psychology of education at the University of Montreal. He
was assigned to educational work in the archdiocese and was a
supervisor for two years. In September, 1939, he founded St.
Joseph's Teachers College in Montreal, and he was principal
of that institution for the next twenty-three years. In 1942,
Father Carter was named Newman chaplain at McGill University in Montreal, a position he held for fifteen years, along
with his work at St. Joseph's Teachers College. He also had two
terms as national Newman chaplain.

In 1946, Archbishop Charbonneau appointed Father Carter

to the seven-man Montreal Catholic School Board. He served on that board for fifteen years, right up to the historic day when Cardinal Léger replaced all the priests on the board with laymen. The work of the board had increased to such an extent that in 1961 it had an operating budget of sixty million dollars.

The combination of three key positions—principal of St. Joseph's Teachers College, Newman chaplain at McGill University, and member of the Montreal Catholic School Board—suggests that Father Carter was the key man in education for the English-speaking Catholics in the Province of Quebec, and such was certainly the case. He was made a canon, and in 1961 the Archbishop of Quebec, Primate of Canada, invited Canon Carter to help in the founding of St. Lawrence O'Toole College in Quebec, a classical college for English-speaking Catholics.

Throughout these busy years, Canon Carter had been studying the modern catechetical movement, and he had become an expert on this aspect of religious education. When the important International Study Week on Missionary Catechetics was held at Eichstätt in Germany, in 1960, Canon Carter, with a mandate from the English-speaking bishops of Canada, was present to observe the formulation of conclusions that would influence the whole future of catechetics. They were principles to which he was already dedicated. Within months he had incorporated the "Eichstätt principles" into a book on which he already had worked for some years, *The Modern Challenge to Religious Education* (Sadlier, 1961). The book had as its subtitle: "God's Message and Our Response." Johannnes Hofinger, S.J., internationally known authority on catechetics, hailed the book as "America's first kerygmatic manual of catechetics," and he recommended it, in an interview in *America* (December 2, 1961), as "*the* catechetical manual of our times for America."

On December 2, 1961, Canon Carter was appointed Auxiliary Bishop of London, Ontario. He was consecrated on February 2, 1962, in Notre Dame Church, Montreal, by Cardinal Léger. His brother had been consecrated a bishop in that same church by Cardinal Léger exactly five years earlier, to the very day.

His brother, Most Reverend Alexander Carter, D.D., Bishop of Sault Ste Marie, was a co-consecrator, with the Bishop of London, Most Reverend John C. Cody. The Archbishop of Quebec, Most Reverend Maurice Roy, Primate of Canada, delivered a sermon in French, and the Coadjutor Archbishop of Toronto, Most Reverend Philip Pocock, spoke on behalf of Canada's English-speaking Catholics.

It was in March, 1963, that I visited Bishop Carter at his house in Windsor, Ontario, across the river from Detroit, for the following interview. I knew the tall, impressive bishop as a man of wit and keen intellect. I expected some penetrating observations about the Council, and I was not disappointed.

QUESTION

How did the first session of the Council look to you, Your Excellency? As a newly consecrated bishop, did you feel somewhat like a "back bencher"?

BISHOP CARTER

As you must know, any manifestation of applause or disapproval was outlawed at the study sessions of the Council. At times, however, the cardinal-president for the day had some difficulty in restraining the Fathers from spontaneous outbursts. Moreover, they began almost inevitably in the furthest reaches of the Council chamber, way down near the massive doors that lead to the square. I must confess that this was where I was seated, closer perhaps to the fountains in St. Peter's Square than to the table of the presidents. I had been consecrated only eight months at the opening of the Council, and, although I was already fifty years of age, I had a little of the feeling of being a spectator and an observer in this mighty drama as well as a participant and a Father of the Council.

Other prelates whom you have interviewed, Father Abbott, due to their exalted position, long experience and great influence, have looked at the Council from a position of eminence. I assure you that I looked at it with the sensation that I was looking up, not down. I am fully cognizant of, and in agreement with, the developing concept of the collegial aspects of the episcopacy, but one cannot completely submerge one's human reactions.

QUESTION

You brought to the Council a background of considerable experience in the field of religious education. I have been wondering what you thought about the work of the Council in that connection.

BISHOP CARTER

I was thrilled—there is no other word for it—moved to the very core of my being, to witness here on the grand scale, on the cosmic level of the universal Church, essentially the same struggle, the same desire for communication with both Catholic and non-Catholic in which I had been privileged to participate during the previous twenty-five years of my priesthood.

Before I went to the Council, I was told that Cardinal Ritter had assured a gathering of teachers in St. Louis that "this would be a catechetical Council." At the time, I wondered what he meant. I was not long left in the dark either about the accuracy of this statement or about the fullness of its meaning. For an old war-horse of the catechetical renewal —I think I may call myself a pioneer in the field in North America—the similarity of the issues was striking.

QUESTION

Your book, The Modern Challenge to Religious Education, *proved that you are the leading authority on the catechetical movement in North America. You are the ideal person to explain the connection between what has been going on in the catechetical field and what is happening at the Second Vatican Council.*

BISHOP CARTER

Well, let me put it like this. In the catechetical revival we have felt that the major problem of modern religious teaching is not primarily one of concern with greater and greater accuracy. We recognize and profit by the great theological advancement which has taken place since the early days of the Church. But catechetics is not theology. It is based upon theology and profits by theology, but it is not primarily the technical and scientific formulation of doctrines. It is, above all, a transmission of the Good News of salvation, which is to clarify the mind of man, of course, but above all, to reach his heart and the totality of life so that in accordance with the realization of the mission of Christ Himself "they may have life, and have it more abundantly."

After the Reformation, in a welter of inaccuracies, of doubts and even of heresies, which rose within the Christian world, it was necessary to spend a great deal of time and effort on precise formulation. Some of this had to be presented to the teachers of religion, even on the lower levels of education. But with the Council of Trent, the doubts concerning main matters, particularly about justification and interpretation of the Bible, etc., were laid to rest, and the Catholic world was once more in the sure possession of the truth. Unfortunately, the weapon of polemics, the necessary formulation of the period, became increasingly the sole method of teaching religion, even to children, and the warmth of the faith, the vivid portrayal of the personality of Christ, the sense of living His mysteries in the liturgy, the need to know of the love of God and to respond to it with love, most—if not all—of these facets were obscured in an exaggerated philosophical and conceptual overstatement of the purely intellectual issues.

Shortly after the turn of this century, a great cry went up, most notably in the countries of Central Europe, demanding a return to the concept of Christian living in the communication of religious education, as a reaction against this exaggerated conceptualism. Father Joseph Jungmann eventually used the word "kerygmatics" (I prefer the expression "Scripture-liturgical approach") and it became synonymous with the renewal. Its essence was to insist upon the concept of communication, of dealing with children in whatever state we found them psychologically, and of making people aware of the value of religion in their lives, in whatever agonizing problems they might have to face. We might say that it was based upon a number of facets, but it was essentially simple in its approach. It was a movement of restoration, of renewal, not an innovation or a fad.

QUESTION

It involved, too, didn't it, a return to the preaching of Christ and the Apostles as we find it in Holy Scripture?

BISHOP CARTER

Its basis was an insistence upon the Good News of salvation in terms of God's intervention in human history, which meant, of course, a return to the Scriptures. But it could not be satisfied with a study of Scripture as history. It was rather the preparation to lead the Christian to relive the mysteries of the life of the Saviour in his own life in the continuous and personalized pattern of the Redemption.

It is often said that the kerygmatic approach has a dual aspect. The first is what God has done for us, which means, of course, an understanding of His loving intervention in the lives of men and, in particular, in our own lives. The second aspect is the reaction which we must produce if the Redemption is to be carried on through every person in each generation, namely, that we must return love for love. As I like to say when I am discussing this before teachers, "there is no adequate response for love save love."

QUESTION

In other words, we should present Christian doctrine not simply as a collection of dogmas we must believe and commandments we must observe and tracts on grace and the sacraments that we must use, but it should be taught as a life to be lived, in terms of God's loving design for us and our response.

BISHOP CARTER

This is exactly the point. The Council was doing the very selfsame thing. As everyone knows, the first debate of the Council was on the liturgy. What was the view of the majority, which became practical unanimity before it was over? An overwhelming desire to involve the people of God in worship.

The conflict of opinion, if you might call it that, was primarily over the language of the liturgy. There were those who felt that any loss of the Latin language would be a blow to unity and, in the same way, a derogation of the tradition of the Church. Some Fathers seemed to be saying that it didn't matter whether the people understood, God did. It was a little like the people who used to say about learning formulas by heart without understanding: "It does not matter whether the children understand it now; they will understand it later." The contrary opinions very soon made themselves heard and carried the day. They were all based on the position that what is important in the liturgy is to involve the people of God; there was no use in imagining that reciting prayers in a language which was incomprehensible was necessarily more pleasing to God, more intellectually satisfying or more conducive to true worship.

One of the great beauties of the Council was the willingness of every Father to learn and, if necessary, to change his position in view of cogent arguments. Many of us had held a fond and lingering attachment to the Latin of our youth, of our seminary days, of our years of Masses and ceremonies. But when we heard a bishop from one of the Iron Curtain countries saying that, in view of his political situation, the liturgy was the only chance he had of reaching his people and that, for him, the use of the vernacular was a matter of spiritual life or death; when we heard the bishops of Japan speaking through their representative and telling us that any Western language could constitute more of a difficulty than an asset in the evangelization of this great people; when we listened to North American bishops pleading for a reform of the breviary in a fashion calculated to nourish the spiritual life of the priests, the fears of those who, in all sincerity, wanted no change in the universal status of Latin were alleviated and a permissive attitude was taken which led to the semiunanimous acceptance of the first chapter on the liturgy.

The same was true of the now famous debate on the document called *De Fontibus Revelationis*. It would be, in my opinion, a mistake to think that this was primarily a doctrinal struggle or argument. Some orators tried to put it on this basis, but I think most of the Fathers agreed that the problem was not one of accuracy of doctrine but, once more, a question of communication. Why, said more than one of the Fathers, why accentuate the differences? Why spend our time honing a weapon which is already so sharp, namely, our theological positions? The first twenty Councils of the Church had been devoted to this acuity of our theology. In this time and under these circumstances, could we remain aloof from the agony of man involved in his own destiny, puzzled by his own scientific achievements, burdened by a false philosophy or none at all? Did we not have to reach into his life and communicate with him on a new psycho-theological plane? Had not the Holy Father himself given us this as our watchword for the Council?

The accusations leveled against the first draft of this document were principally that it was too scholastic, exaggeratedly intellectualistic, filled with terminology which, however accurate, was not too comprehensible and, above all, did not reach into the marrow of the bones. It added little to our message, our communication. The events of the 21st and the 22nd of November are too well known for me to rehearse here, but we can recall that on the 21st almost two-thirds of the Fathers of the Council desired that this *schema* be totally reconstructed and on the 22nd the Holy Father intervened to support this position, in view not only of the overwhelming majority which had expressed this view, but also of the serious considerations against it which had been brought forward.

Many of us came out of that session of the 22nd of November with a sense of exhilaration that can hardly be described. If I may inject a personal note, I rode home in the bus to our hotel that day and I said to one of the Council theologians sitting beside me: "I am convinced that historians will write that today marked the end of the Post-Tridentine era." And you can see from what I am saying that the parallel with catechetics is striking. Once more, as in the case of *De Fontibus,* it is not a question of anything inaccurate in the formulations which have dominated the catechetical scene. They are incomplete and lacking often in proper stress, but it is mostly that we cannot remain with formulations. They may be there as guides, but they cannot be the whole of our catechetical teaching. They can certainly not be the starting point nor even the essential burden of our message. As with the *schema* which was provocatively entitled *De Fontibus Revelationis* and is now called *De Revelatione Divina,* we have to get back to the "heart of the matter."

QUESTION

What you have described was certainly an example of Council Fathers striving to achieve the aggiornamento *that Pope John stressed when he convoked the Council. Were there many notable occasions of this* aggiornamento, *or updating of the communication of the Christian message?*

BISHOP CARTER

Yes, I believe there were many other examples. I give only a few. The big objection about the document *De Ecclesia* was again that it presented to the world a juridical notion of the Church. Once again, outstanding prelates in the Church rose to say that, of course, there was no lack of accuracy in this document but it did not get over to the people, in the Church or out of it. A long discussion took place, for example, on the question of the concept of the coextension of the Church with the Mystical Body. But was it, once more, a question of juridical definition of the Church or the Mystical Body? Was a restatement of this juridical notion all that important? Could it not be left safely to theologians? Many felt that it could, and that what we were looking for was an image of the Church to project to the world which would make it in effect the image of the continuing presence of Christ among us. Why exacerbate other believers in Christ by insisting upon their removal from us? Why not try to find ground in which we could share a common identity and thereby move a step closer to Christ and to some form of common brotherhood? A great cardinal rose to say: "I, for one, would not dare to say that someone who has been baptized, who lives in the grace of Christ, is not—in some way—incorporated into Him." And another bishop exclaimed: "This manner of speech is not worthy of the Church if she is truly a mother. What mother ever said of her child whom she has borne and raised in her love —even if for some unfortunate reason he is not with his brethren under the paternal roof—'you are not a member of my family.' "

This was the spirit of the discussion, and it seemed to me that it was completely the spirit of modern catechesis.

QUESTION

I personally do not feel this difficulty, but I raise it here because I know that some others in the Church would do so. They would suggest here, I think, that this spirit you describe may perhaps be rushing rashly beyond the truth of theology to embrace something that is founded merely on hopes and sentiments.

BISHOP CARTER

I realize that what I have said up to now may very easily give that impression. It is not the impression I wish to leave, however. On the contrary, I believe that modern catechesis is firmly based on true theology. Let me try to explain this in terms of what I have already said concerning the movement of the catechetical revival or, if you prefer, the kerygmatic approach.

It would be a great mistake to think that we are leaving sound and even profound theology when we take up this attitude. For example, let us contemplate for a moment the concept of what is called salvation history but really means the emphasis upon God's intervention in man's destiny. One of the basic theses of theology is to the effect that God, by His absolute power, could have saved man without becoming incarnate. By a simple decree, God could have wiped away the sin of Adam and the following sins of mankind. He could have revealed His mercy in a set of formulas surrounded by "whereases," but we know that God did not choose this particular procedure. He began His merciful intervention with the rehabilitation of the first man, continued it in an obscure but nevertheless effective fashion all through what is known as the Old Testament, brought it to full light in the appearance of our Lord upon the earth, and then made it secure and permanent by the special gift of the Holy Spirit, in order that we would have the necessary light to understand it and interpret it in the fullness of the ages. These are facts, events; they are concrete, not abstract. The Incarnation itself or, to use the proper theological expression, the hypostatic union is a concrete thing. It is a physical—in the proper sense of the term—manifestation of the Divinity. God condescended to our weakness and established a juncture with us through the Sacred Humanity of our Lord. He used our own flesh, and so it was possible for the angels to proclaim to the shepherds, not a conceptual formulation of divine mercy and goodwill, but a concrete realization: "Behold, I bring you good tidings of great joy, that shall be to all the people; for this day is born to you a Saviour, who is Christ the Lord, in the city of David. And this shall be a sign unto you: You shall find the infant wrapped in swaddling clothes and laid in a manger." There could be hardly anything more concrete than this. And then we saw the fulfillment of this concrete intervention in the life, the preaching and, finally, the triumphal death and resurrection of the Saviour as it unfolded before the eyes of the world. And we have only to note the use the Apostles made of this history, of these events, to realize that it is the center of the salvific history of God with man.

QUESTION

There certainly are deep biblical foundations for the present trends in the catechetical movement. What do you think the Council might do to help bring the people in contact with those biblical riches?

BISHOP CARTER

Again, let us consider the insistence upon the use of Scripture which characterizes the catechetical renewal. If I may return to the Council, everyone has remarked upon the inspiration derived from seeing the Holy Bible carried daily by a bishop the length of St. Peter's and placed upon the altar, open, in full view of the assembled Fathers, so that everyone would know that the word of God presided in our deliberations. This stress, within the Council, upon the importance of the Scriptures as the basis of the deliberations of the teaching Church is exactly reflected in the similar preoccupation of the modern teacher of religion. We believe in a real dynamism of Holy Scripture—above any human means or human study and conclusions.

Perhaps the catechetical approach can best be summed up by a remark made by the esteemed scriptural scholar Father Barnabas Mary Ahern when he spoke to us at one of our episcopal meetings. At the end of his lucid and scholarly treatment of the new trends in scriptural study, in a touching gesture of faith, he concluded with something that reminded us of St. Thomas' assertion that "what he had written was as straw." Father Ahern said: "Your Excellencies, I want you to understand one thing. If I could be given a tape recording containing every word that our Lord spoke and rolls of film showing His every action, I should be delighted. But if I had to choose between these things and the New Testament just as we have it today, I would—without hesitation—choose the New Testament. This is the way God wanted us to have His revelation. We have the very power of His wisdom in these words."

Modern catechesis maintains, as the Church has always maintained, that there is something over and above a literary or historical study, that "the word of God is not bound," "that man lives out of every word that proceeds from the mouth of God," that the Scripture has a vital force of its own to bring the believer to the person of our Lord.

As a result, we maintain that some of the past practices of the classroom have to be changed. Scripture should not be brought in to prove that the formulas are accurate, in a sort of "now-see-I-was-right" attitude, but as the very heart of our teaching. We begin with what Christ said and did. We may legitimately draw conclusions from them, but this has to be the central point. Would you say that this is poor theology? It is the heart of what we call the Christocentric attitude, which is the only true basis of sound theology. "Everyone who has listened to the Father, and has learned, comes to me" (John 6:45). God Himself has made His Son the center of His revelation and the center of our spiritual lives. It cannot be otherwise in our teaching. "Now this is everlasting life, that they may know thee, the only true God, and him whom thou hast sent, Jesus Christ" (John 17:3).

The third aspect of catechetics that I mentioned, namely the continuous and personalized pattern of the Redemption, is also a key point. If you prefer to call it the liturgy, you may do so, but it has the richest and warmest of theological foundations. Once more, it is basic theology to understand that, although the death of our Lord upon the cross was infinite in its grace and merit, His redemptive action has to be applied to the soul of every man in each succeeding generation. How strongly St. Paul worded this when he says: "What is lacking of the sufferings of Christ I fill up in my flesh." What could be wanting to the infinite sufferings of Christ, except that we make our free compliance and our use of this available treasure? This, in short, is the meaning of the Church—Christ with us, Christ continued in time and space, Christ in each generation.

Modern catechesis insists that the people, particularly the little people, have to realize they must live the mysteries of Christ in their own lives. To show how Scripture and liturgy are the twin pillars of the temple of modern catechesis, I may be permitted—I am sure you will not object, Father Abbott— to borrow an Ignatian idea. In his meditations on the life of Christ, Ignatius insists upon a very vivid composition of place. We are advised by our Jesuit retreat masters to use the formula "I was there." With this technique, we try to examine all the details of the scene we are contemplating as if we were physically present.

This is more than just a pious technique. It approximates very real truth. "I was there" because Christ was there. Where the Head is, there are the members. In the events of Scripture, in the projection of time, "I was there." But it is equally true that He is here. He is here because He is joined to His members. He is wherever there is someone who lives with the life of Christ. This is the true concept of the liturgy: Christ living again in us and with us and worshiping the Father in us and with us. And we bring little children to realize that their contribution is great, irreplaceable, sublime. They are living again the mysteries of Christ, His birth, His growing up, His fasting, His suffering and His triumph.

Finally, who can say that the insistence upon love is anything but theological? One of the small catechisms has a primary question: "Why did God make [create] me?" Answer: "God made me to know and to love and to serve Him in this world, and to be happy with Him in eternity." Now, this is not false. It is true that it is highly conceptualized and hardly useful for children before the middle grades at the earliest, but at least, properly explained, it can be made to stand up. But it falls short of the most important theological consideration of creation.

God, the Perfect One, *ipsum esse subsistens* (subsistent being itself), is complete and completely happy within Himself. In His eternal contemplation of Himself, in His eternal love of Himself we find the divine processions, and the life of the Three is One. He could not, then, by any imagining have any need outside Himself. Consequently, He could only have created out of His divine goodness—out of love.

But take the operative word "serve" in the catechism definition. Doesn't it give you an impression of rendering service to God? Doesn't it lead imperceptibly to the widely held notion among Catholics that, in some way, God needed our labor and created us to "do a job" for Him?

How much do I prefer—how much more theological I find —a tiny illustrated catechetical booklet for very young children. It has to do with creation. One "illustration" is a double page, completely black. In white type in the corner we find this: "Nothing was everywhere except love. So God just made the world out of love!" This is a profound theological insight, and yet a child can and will be illumined by it.

Again, although we are taught that the proximate reason for the Incarnation and Redemption was man's sin, we must remember that, just as He first loved us in creation, He completed that love by His intervention and redemption. The only way in which a Christian can be involved totally is through a return of love. Fear can lead a man to some involvement, to some compliance. It may be the beginning of wisdom, but it is not the totality of wisdom. Only love can bring a Christian to the high point of perfection and of performance.

QUESTION

You have gone to the heart of the kerygmatic approach. Some priests and people I know complain that the word "kerygmatic" is too difficult. I tell them that the word kerygma *means the "heralded message" of essential Christianity, but they wish we would use something simpler. If they do not get a new word, at least they should be reassured by what you have said and what the Council is doing about the movement itself.*

BISHOP CARTER

The kerygmatic approach, or, if you prefer, the modern catechetical movement insists upon this great theological truth that God loves us, and it demands in return that the fire of love be kindled in the hearts of all, of little children as well as of their seniors.

I think it is a great mistake to imagine that the kerygmatic approach is something which is lacking in theological depth and insight or something which is almost anti-intellectual. My conviction is that, far to the contrary, if children are brought up in this greater and more personalized knowledge of Christ, they will find such an interest in religion that when the time comes that their minds are sufficiently developed and capable of other depths, they will have the desire to achieve a greater intellectual insight into theology, and the idea of "faith searching for understanding" will be more prevalent than it is today.

I repeat that the catechetical movement is only the reflection of the Council. The impression may have got abroad that the Fathers were in a sort of emotional or "communications" ecstasy. There are those who felt that the ecumenical aspect was exaggerated to the point of depreciating theology. In my humble opinion, nothing could be further from the truth. Just as I feel that the catechetical movement is based upon sound theology and asceticism and mysticism, so I feel that the theological considerations of the Council are very profound indeed. There are, perhaps, new insights; they are not quite the technical insights of the past, but they are nevertheless profoundly theological. And so, of course, is ecumenism. It is an understanding of theology, not necessarily a formulation of it. It is the understanding that "if any man *says* that he loves God, whom he does not see, while he does not love his brother, whom he does see, the same is a liar."

So, Father Abbott, perhaps I could close as I began. I do not know how many times a text of Scripture kept recurring to me: "It is good for us to be here; if thou wilt, let us make here three tabernacles, one for thee, one for Moses, and one for Elias," because, far from finding any lack of nourishment in this magnificent first session, I found that we had touched upon the fulfillment of the Law and the Prophets by a fuller discovery of our Lord Himself. And this is what the apostle seeks on any level.

Bishop Carter is kept busy with many episcopal duties, and he is called upon to give much of his time to consultations on educational matters. The day I visited him, the president of one university and the vice president of another came to see him. But Bishop Carter has kept up his interest in the catechetical movement and intends to keep on doing so.

In his book he dealt frankly and effectively with the traditionalism that he calls "one of the most astounding things about the Church in North America." The "offhand approach to things," the "lack of interest in detail" and the reputation for "getting things done quickly but not necessarily thoroughly" are thought by Europeans to characterize the United States and Canada, yet, he pointed out in the book, "probably nowhere in the world is the observance of Church customs and laws as strict as in the strongly Catholic areas of North America." All this, he felt, was to the good, "saving certain exaggerations," but he wondered whether this traditionalism was working to the benefit of the Church in the teaching of religion. When the book was published, Father Hofinger said in the *America* interview that Canon Carter would be heard for what he had to say about North America. What he had to say was that North America had not been in the forefront of the catechetical revival, and that "the false impression that the catechetical revival is an attempt at innovation is one which must be corrected at once if we in North America are to benefit by the success and experience of those spearheading the catechetical movement abroad during the past half-century." Today we may add that he will be heard indeed— all the more so now that he is a bishop, and now that the Second Vatican Council has taken place.

XI

ADAPTATION

AND PROGRESS

Julius Cardinal Doepfner, Archbishop of Munich and Freising, West Germany, heads one of the largest dioceses in the world— 1,943,000 Catholics out of a total population of 2,357,000. Munich, of course, is in one of the most Catholic parts of the world, Bavaria. When I met the cardinal at his house in Munich, a splendid palace on Kardinal-Faulhaber-Strasse, I was impressed by the vigor and power of the prelate. Not yet fifty years old, he is tall, dark-haired and broad-shouldered. He has the build and carriage of an athlete. When he entered the room where I was waiting, I thought immediately of a heavyweight boxer I had known years ago in America. Later that day, I learned that the cardinal is a mountain climber. I was reminded of a certain Father Ratti, who was also a mountain climber and a cardinal, and later a Pope (Pius XI).

Cardinal Doepfner was born on August 26, 1913, in Hausen, in the Diocese of Würzburg, Germany. He was ordained to the priesthood on October 29, 1939. After higher studies in Rome, at the Gregorian University and the Germanicum, famous old house of studies for German priests, he received a doctorate in theology.

On his return to Germany, Father Doepfner was assigned to parish work at Grosswallstadt near Aschaffenburg. Eventually, he became parish priest at Schweinfurt. In 1946, he was appointed vice rector at the Würzburg seminary. On August 11,

1948, Pope Pius XII named him Bishop of Würzburg. He was only thirty-five years old when he took possession of his see, two months later. He was the youngest member of the hierarchy in Europe.

Bishop Doepfner found himself head of a diocese that had some of its parishes in the Soviet Zone of East Germany. There were about 900,000 Catholics in a population of one and a half million. The record shows that he worked and prayed, and urged his people to work and pray, for "greater unity of faith among us." He succeeded in winning the cooperation of Protestants; they opened their churches for the celebration of Mass in towns and villages that lacked a Catholic church. One of his frequent themes in sermons during those days was the call for all Christians to work together against "the anti-Christian forces of the world." Now, as in his early days as a priest, he promoted Christian social action among his people, especially in the trade-union movement.

On January 15, 1957, Bishop Doepfner was transferred from Würzburg to Berlin. On March 25 of that year, he was enthroned as Bishop of Berlin in St. Sebastian's Church, in the Soviet sector of the city. As Bishop of Berlin, a diocese standing like an island in the Communist world and partly submerged under Communist control, he carried a burden of worry that was unique. I remember writing an editorial for the May 30, 1959, issue of *America*, pointing out that one of the bishop's problems had been that for a year East Germany's Communist government had barred him from visiting his parishes in the Soviet Zone. In January of that year, the bishop inaugurated a religious program over Radio Free Berlin directed especially to Soviet Zone Catholics. The cardinal—he was a cardinal by this time, having been elevated by Pope John at the consistory of December 15, 1958— was on the air himself every second week, denouncing Communist trials in which, he said, "Soviet Zone Catholics are unlawfully deprived of their liberty."

The cardinal had been banned from the Soviet sector, of course, because he had been so vigorous and forthright in condemning Communist tactics, especially in the arrests of priests, nuns and laymen in East Berlin and East Germany. He had complained that no charges were made against many that were arrested, and he revealed that repeated efforts to discover reasons for the arrests had been fruitless. In March, 1958, he said in a sermon that "the first goal of those who oppress the Church in large areas of the world today is to loosen and then destroy all ties with Rome." He spoke out against Communist attempts to substitute atheistic ceremonies for the Christian sacraments, and added: "We cannot permit our children to suffer from this feeble mockery of religion."

The cardinal had come to be called "the bishop of two worlds," because his diocese was split between the Free World and Communist-controlled East Germany. On July 3, 1961, he was promoted to head the great Archdiocese of Munich. When I came to see him, I was thinking of the sermon he had delivered at his installation ceremony in Berlin, in 1957, when he stressed how urgent it was that Christians close ranks, whatever their denominations might be, against Communism's threat to Christianity. In the interview that follows, I learned that his thinking about the Church's confrontation with Communism had deepened and broadened.

QUESTION

Is it Your Eminence's opinion that the first session of the Second Vatican Council was important for developing attitudes and trends?

CARDINAL DOEPFNER

It was in the nature of things, and therefore it was to be expected, that definite directions and various schools of opinion would develop. It was a natural thing to have happen in the course of a certain initial period. Without a certain development of groups, like the formation of parties in a parliament, it would be hardly possible to arrive at a common decision in such a large gathering—nearly two and a half thousand voting members! Naturally, for good reasons, the business setup of the Council knows no divisions or parties. Nevertheless, it is only natural that those who hold similar ideas should group themselves together more closely. In the end, the possibility that a Council Father might speak in the name of a group of Council Fathers became a reality—in fact, an organized reality—and frequent use was made of it.

One might be curious to know which tendencies would be crystallized as a result. One must remember, however, that concrete necessities in different parts of the Church are very different. Take just one example. In some countries, the Church has lived together for centuries with other confessions and has worked with them in fruitful fashion in many areas of culture, politics, economy, social action and education. By every standard, she has nevertheless completely preserved her own independence. In other regions, which up to the present have been reputed as solidly Catholic, the Church sees herself today as exposed to an increasing influence of foreign ways of thinking. Here and there, those foreign ways are seen as an actual danger for her existence. Accordingly, requests and expectations presented to the Second Vatican Council differed notably in this regard. Some sought assistance in working out more and more adaptation; others expected more preservative measures as a protection against what they discerned as a threatened loss of something pertaining to their very substance. Some consider that it is of primary importance to achieve a renovation in practical preaching and the care of souls. Others look more for renewal in the form of making sharp demarcation between Catholic doctrine and surrounding false concepts. Which of these tendencies would get the upper hand? That was the question many were asking.

Here is where the first period of the Council proved to be of decisive significance. The results in the selection of members of the commissions had already indicated the direction that would be taken in the future. The treatment of the first *schema, De Sacra Liturgia,* confirmed it. The tendencies for pastoral renovation got the upper hand.

Of course, Pope John XXIII, by his talks held shortly before (September 11 and October 11), had given a decisive impetus in this direction. He had explained, for instance, that even the teaching office of the Church was obliged to serve a pastoral goal. The lively echo which these words of the Pope aroused shows how close to their hearts the bishops had the question of pastoral renovation.

One can say, therefore, that a decisive result of the first period of the Council was the elevating of pastoral renovation to become the Council's chief aim, so that the Church would be truly the "Light of the Nations" and would also show present-day humanity the way to salvation. At the same time, various opinions were proposed as to how this goal would be best reached, whether it should be more through renewed precision of traditional teaching and discipline or through organic and wider development of this same tradition. Arguments for both tendencies were proposed very clearly and often not without sharpness. However, if one looks at the result of the various votes, the latter of the two directions I have referred to can claim a decisive majority.

QUESTION

Is the debate on the fonts of revelation (or on revelation, simply) merely a matter of terminology, or is it more substantial and crucial?

CARDINAL DOEPFNER

Many rumors give the impression that the debate in the Council over the "fonts of revelation" turned only on the question whether we are to accept one or two sources of revelation. Since the final source of all revelation can only be the one God, such a disputation appears as a mere battle of words.

In reality, much more was involved, even if it was not immediately noticeable on account of the abstractness of the technical theological expressions. The question at issue was that of bringing divine revelation to the people of our day in the most efficient and emphatic form. That revelation, especially the word of God as written in Holy Scripture, is for their salvation, of course. We bishops hope for a second spring of spiritual life for the faithful, and we look for it to come from a newly revived veneration and evaluation of the word of God contained in Holy Scripture. We look for it to be something like the emergence of Eucharistic adoration in the Middle Ages, with its notable enrichment of the Church's life of faith.

Naturally, in this connection, there was discussion of the relation between the teaching office, Holy Scripture and vocal tradition. It was not easy to find a form of expression which would emphasize the normative significance of Holy Scripture for the Church's teaching office, theological knowledge and the spiritual life (of priests and laity) in desirable fashion, while still keeping an organic connection with existing doctrinal statements. But the chief goal of the *schema* had to be, and must remain, the awakening and deepening of understanding of Holy Scripture as well as renovation of the Church's preaching through more intensive use of the riches which are found in the Bible.

QUESTION

Do you strongly favor the trend toward bishops' having jurisdiction over liturgical matters in regional or national conferences?

CARDINAL DOEPFNER

In answering that question, one should first clarify what liturgical matters are concretely concerned. There are certain essential elements of the liturgy which must be preserved uniformly in the entire Church—for instance, the essential form of celebration of the Holy Eucharist. Matters of that kind cannot be submitted to the free decision of individual bishops' conferences. Many other questions—for instance, the adaptation of certain rites to national or regional conditions, use of the national language in certain parts of the liturgy, etc.—naturally call for a uniform regulation, *not* for the whole Church *but* for what suits a certain nation or region. Questions of that kind can and should be submitted to the competence of the corresponding bishops' conferences for a decision.

QUESTION

Are there special problems in the discussion about the relationship between Pope and bishops? How do you think this discussion should develop at the next session, Your Eminence? Is there something to be learned in this matter from the experience of bishops, from tradition, etc.?

CARDINAL DOEPFNER

As you know, the First Vatican Council was not able to carry the questions about the episcopal office to a conclusion. Ever since then, the question about the relationship between the Pope and the bishop's office has always been recurring. Frequently, an actual contrast was seen between the two powers, and many feared that, through the (historically conditioned) one-sided emphasis on the power of the primacy at the First Vatican Council, the episcopal power would be pushed into the background. So there was a demand for a plainer dogmatic and canonical elaboration of the bishops' pastoral power.

It would be quite wrong, however, if people were to see in this demand a possibly unconscious or hidden opposition to Rome. Nevertheless, there must be a theoretical and practical elucidation as to exactly how the relationship of the two powers established by Christ is to be understood. The fact is that the episcopal power was not established so that it is exercised by the bishops acting each one for his own diocese. It is also to be exercised for the whole Church, according to the words of our Lord: "Whatever you (plural) bind on earth shall be bound also in heaven; and whatever you (plural) loose on earth shall be loosed also in heaven" (Matt. 18:18). Precisely on this account, the episcopal power would seem to collide with the papal power, which likewise fully and immediately reaches all dioceses (Matt. 16:19: "Whatever thou shalt bind on earth shall be bound in heaven, and whatever thou shalt loose on earth shall be loosed in heaven"). How, then, are we to find a harmonizing unity in this matter?

Summing up, I could answer the first part of your question as follows: With regard to the relationship of papal and episcopal power, these questions come up for discussion: How can the power of the bishops be more exactly understood, whether it concern the single dioceses entrusted to them or the entire episcopacy over the entire Church? How does this episcopal power fit into a unity with the papal power? What conclusions are we to draw from this for the legal structure of the Church?

Today, of course, we cannot yet make any prediction as to how future deliberations of the Council will treat this theme. However, in one form or another, the Council's discussions will lead to a clearer understanding of the unity of both powers. Christ confided the government of the Church not to one Apostle alone but to the twelve. It was not committed to twelve officials independent of one another, but, rather, the twelve Apostles exercised the pastoral power over the whole Church as a unified college. At the head of this college stands Peter, who represents and guarantees its unity (and thus the unity of the whole Church). The same holds for the college of bishops with the Pope at its head.

That a fruitful cooperation of episcopal and papal power in unity and for the good of the Church is possible is shown by the Council's preparation, convocation and development up to now. Already through its mere existence it refutes the assertions of those who thought that the papal power would predominate over the episcopal so that no council could again take

place. Certainly we can expect that the constructive cooperation of the bishops in the government of the entire Church
that was here manifested will continue in some form even
after the Council, more effective than ever. A way is thus
opened up by which experiences in individual dioceses and
provinces can benefit God's entire people much more rapidly
and comprehensively than is now the case.

QUESTION

*What do you foresee as developments in the idea of regional
conferences of bishops?*

CARDINAL DOEPFNER

The cooperation of bishops on a regional plane is something
that is already deeply anchored in the Church's tradition.
Think of the significance of the regional councils in the latter
days of antiquity and the Middle Ages! We can think of the
provincial councils of Carthage (418) and Orange (529),
which were confirmed by the Pope and became valid for the
whole Church, or the important Lateran Synod under Pope
Martin I (649). Our present Code of Canon Law recognizes
the form of provincial or plenary councils.

In modern states since the last century, it has often been
necessary that the bishops of a region should quickly work out
a coordinated plan of action on definite questions. For this
purpose, a conference of bishops seemed to be particularly
suited which would be assembled without the formalities required for councils. In many countries, conferences have
already been established. It would be desirable to have this
institution of the bishops' conference crystallized in Canon
Law.

The idea of the bishops' conferences should be further
developed. Up to the present, where they occur, they serve
chiefly for consultation and coordination of action. In the
future, besides this, their primary function, they should be
able to establish an obligatory law for the whole territory in

certain instances which should be clearly defined. There are concerns which, from the nature of the case or for the sake of uniform action of the Church within a specified nation, should by all means be regulated for an entire territory or region. I am thinking here, for instance, of the introduction of official catechisms for the different types of schools in a nation, or the already mentioned use of the national language in certain parts of the liturgy.

QUESTION

What will be the role of the laity? What do you recommend that the Council could decide about the function of laymen and laywomen in the Church? In this connection, what about the idea of married people as deacons?

CARDINAL DOEPFNER

In recent decades, lay action has already developed in manifold forms in different countries. The layman is becoming responsible, that is, he is beginning to work actively with the hierarchy so that the Church can fulfill her mission in the world. There are many forms of this active cooperation. It can take place on the individual level or in organizations. These organizations can operate under the immediate direction of the hierarchy or through direction of lay people under control of the hierarchy, or they can operate entirely on their own responsibility in accordance with the general teaching of the Church and their general instructions.

In this matter of the role of the laity, the Council should describe the various aims and tasks and the various possibilities which are proper for lay action. In the main, there are two types of tasks: 1) the *apostolate,* that is to say, the task (in union with the clergy) of bringing supernatural salvation closer to mankind and preparing the way for the task, that is to say, producing, before all else, the conditions for a favorable and fruitful acceptance of the Christian message among all groups of society and all walks of life; 2) *charitable activity,* without which an apostolate that would be worthy of belief and successful cannot long exist, that is to say, assistance to all who through sickness, old age, difficult social relationships or in other ways come into physical or spiritual distress.

Among the special tasks of the laity belongs the apostolate of the environment, e.g., the apostolate of workers in industrial plants. Laymen have access to areas which are often closed to the clergy.

There are tasks that are particularly fitting for men, e.g., the realization of an atmosphere favorable for Christianity in public life (the state, the local community, the economy, etc.). Other activities concern particularly women and mothers: Christian education of children, especially where, for example, on account of a state monopoly of schools, the clergy cannot immediately reach children and youth.

As to how far the question of a married diaconate for the entire Church will be discussed in this connection (in some Oriental churches it has always existed) is still not determined. I would endorse a regional experiment, especially in areas that are poor in priests. Of course, strong objections can be raised against this, but I hope they may be surmounted.

QUESTION

What about the relations between Church and State? Can the Council do something to help development of the more modern ideas (as, for example, in the United States)?

CARDINAL DOEPFNER

This question of the relation between Church and State was something that was also considered in the preparatory work for the Council. Of course, the Council can establish only general principles. The application of these principles will have to differ from state to state.

It would be a great advance if states and politicians, especially those that are farther removed from the Catholic Church, could come to see that the Church in the present-day

world is not concerned with the defense and zealous mainte-
nance of political positions of power. The Church would rather
contribute to the idea that men in general, and particularly
her own members, should devote themselves to the right
ordering of society and the state so that human freedom and
dignity would be safeguarded and those conditions could be
established which would make possible for all men a life to be
enjoyed in peace and without oppression (the *bonum
commune*).

Certainly in the treatment of this question the most recent
pronouncements of the popes, especially the encyclicals *Mater
et Magistra* and *Pacem in Terris*, can serve as a guiding star.
Modern concepts—such as, for example, the democratic form
of state or the system of division of powers—are clearly indicated as possible principles and entirely congenial to Catholic
teaching. Emphasis is laid on respect for freedom of conscience
on the part of the state. Certainly the Council can proceed
further in the same direction.

The concrete embodiment of these principles in the social
and political relations governing a community will reflect the
complexities of the makeup of its population at a given time.
It must also be determined what possibilities there are for cooperative action with non-Catholic groups and common goals.

QUESTION

*What about relations with non-Catholics? What do you
recommend that Catholic thinking should develop in accordance with the realities of our modern pluralistic society? Can
the Council say something about harmonious living with Protestants, Jews and others? What about the ideas of tolerance,
respect for rights of the individual, freedom of conscience,
etc.?*

CARDINAL DOEPFNER

It is quite logical that you should now propose this question,
for the problem of cooperation of Church and State already

touched upon depends in great measure on a positive solution of this question. In general, it touches on one of the most significant aspects of this Council. From the very time the Council was announced, the Pope's hopeful words aroused fervent expectation inside and outside the Catholic Church that the widespread modern effort for Christian unity might be one of its chief concerns. Even though the Second Vatican Council does not appear as a Council of Union, yet one could say already that it will make a significant step farther along the path toward drawing the various beliefs together. The Council will create important conditions for a better mutual understanding if, for example, it will make authentic pronouncements on the relations of Catholics to non-Catholic Christians and to non-Christians.

The result of such pronouncements will be, in the first instance, a more exact description of the status of non-Catholic Christians in the light of Catholic doctrinal teaching. The differences that divide us, which we now have to suffer on the score of fidelity to God's word, cannot be erased by such pronouncements, but, whereas in the past we often saw only or almost only our differences, today we should emphasize what we have in common. We have nearly a common faith in God, Creator of all and merciful Father who has revealed Himself to us in Christ His Son. We have our common acknowledgment of Christ, His crucifixion and resurrection: the common hope for the coming of the Lord; the common esteem for Holy Scripture; in many cases, even the common recognition of holy baptism and the Holy Eucharist. Because of what we share in common, there are many possibilities for common life and even common work. These similarities must be seen as establishing the starting point for conversation with others, for a common effort to clarify and surmount differences that still exist.

It is chiefly on the basis of these similarities that we can share a common existence with other groups in a pluralistic society. For no matter how far we may conceive the freedom of single groups to extend in a pluralistic society, if we do not aim at union in certain essential, fundamental questions, we cannot hope for a peaceful association. Without a binding recognition of certain common principles—e.g., freedom of conscience, the essential limitation of freedom of individuals for the common good, the general determination to preserve human rights and the building up of society according to the immanent laws of its being, which we Catholics in general usually include under the expression "natural law"—no form of social coexistence, not even of a pluralistic or democratic type, can long exist.

Now, with that, the last two sections of your question are already answered. The Council will have many positive things to say about Catholic coexistence with Protestants, Jews and others. In all this, the Council should not only point to objective similarities but should also ask Catholics to see their own faults. In place of the aversion and spirit of criticism that one sees here and there today, the Council should set the spirit of brotherly openness and devotion to one's fellowman.

The Council will emphasize the spirit of true tolerance. That spirit should not be confused with indifferentism. Rather, it respects freedom of conscience; it remembers that the Lord never wished to impose His teaching with external compulsion but always appealed to inner conversion, to *metanoia*, and worked for the free offering of the human being, an offering which is made in freedom of belief and love.

QUESTION

You have lived in Berlin, Your Eminence, and have had contact with critical situations involving Communists. Could you say something about the need for unity in the Western world against the threat of Communism?

CARDINAL DOEPFNER

The following is to be said, I think, about this delicate question of the Catholic position on Communism. The confrontation with Communism is first of all a spiritual one. The question of the defense of human freedom as opposed to Communism's physical threats through diplomatic and political actions, and eventually through military opposition, does *not* belong to the immediate area of the Church's responsibility. However, the Church is burdened with the spiritual confrontation, because the Communist ideology menaces the Christian message of salvation in its very foundation.

For this spiritual confrontation, the unity of all members of a free society is necessary. However, it is not so easy to achieve this unity. It cannot be reached where similar materialistic principles such as are proper to Communism are made a norm either in theory or in practical life. Hence, in the spiritual battle against Communism, all men and all groups which reject Communism should make every possible effort to draw closer to one another.

Here you run immediately into the question: What spiritual principles are there, after all, which are unmistakably superior to Communism and enable us to surmount it? Here the Church makes the decisive contribution out of her innermost substance, out of her very being, by invoking the message of salvation in Jesus Christ in a world threatened by Communism. Not any and every new ideology will be able to overcome Communism, but only a Christian realism which understands the insufficiency and the suffering of this world. In a word, only that can succeed which reckons with the cross in this world and that knows the cross is God's power for those who believe. Only that power of God gives peace to man, bestows a real hope for a new and better world and assuages the misery of the world we find ourselves in.

Once more I emphasize that we are concerned, first of all, with a spiritual conquest of Communism. That conquest comes not by force, not through diplomacy and politics, but decisively by ensuring that Christ's message is announced so that His power to change hearts becomes fully effective, and men find their way back to the path of the Gospel through faith and insight.

QUESTION

Having seen various crises in Europe, you see the need for adaptation to modern situations by the Church, and you see the need for changes of various kinds. In other parts of the Church there is a certain immobility, opposition to change, reliance upon custom and established procedures, looking to Rome to settle most things of importance, etc. If that spirit were to prevail, would there be a critical situation in the Church?

CARDINAL DOEPFNER

The tension between conservative and progressive positions belongs essentially to the Church, because she must always announce and apply God's message of salvation, which is the same for all times and peoples, to all peoples and times in their special situations. It would be a disservice to the Church if one were to play the two power groups, conservative and progressive, against each other. It is much more important that the two tendencies should work together in harmony. Fundamentally, there is always a necessity for confrontation with new ideas and forms of life and adaptation to them, somewhat after the motto of St. Paul: "Prove all things; hold fast that which is good." But in all this we must keep the connection with tradition so that "progress" will appear as a further organic development of what exists. For this reason, in the further development of doctrine, discipline, liturgy, etc., in the Church, we should always take into consideration the understanding of the faithful, their spiritual preparation for what is new and their readiness to go forward. The starting point for this is very different in different countries. Therefore, the Council should take care to leave the concrete execution of many resolutions to the initiative of individual regions, that is to say, to the bishops' conferences.

We should all be convinced, however, that the Spirit promised by Christ and given to His Church will lead us today upon the right path of adaptation and progress, so that in our time, as in days gone by, the Church can fulfill the task given her by God, namely, to be the "Light of the Nations."

Dynamic is certainly the word to describe Cardinal Doepfner. Realistic is another apt adjective to describe him. Although he presides over such a thoroughly Catholic part of the world as Bavaria, he told me that the vitality of the Catholic Church in the United States was an impressive fact of such proportions that "it commands respect throughout Europe." "One listens with special respect," he said, "when an American bishop speaks at the Second Vatican Council." "The Church in Europe," he added, "has much to learn from the Church in the United States." As I was leaving him, I kept thinking about how much he and other cardinals I had met in Europe were looking forward to the participation of the American bishops in the next session of the Council. As the reader will see in the next interview, Cardinal Doepfner gave me a very explicit message for Cardinal Cushing.

XII

THE SUPREME LAW

OF CHARITY

Richard Cardinal Cushing, Archbishop of Boston, brought Cardinal Bea to Boston College on March 26, 1963. The president of Boston's Catholic university read a citation honoring the head of the Secretariat for Promoting Christian Unity with a degree of Doctor of Civil and Canon Law. In the citation, which he read before a large audience, the Reverend Michael P. Walsh, S.J., touched upon the very essence of Cardinal Cushing: "We dreamed not only of inviting to the heart of our centennial splendor our own beloved Cardinal of Charity, but of summoning to his side the Cardinal of Unity from the City still echoing the voices of the Church in Council. They are here with us in our plenary convocation. Together they symbolize and in their august persons bear witness to the fresh outpouring of apostolic love by which the Holy Spirit forever renews the face of the earth."

When I flew in to Boston that afternoon, the plane circled low over the city. It was clear and sunny. I could see everywhere how the Cardinal of Charity had changed the map with his buildings as much as state and city with their projects. His schools, churches, hospitals, seminaries, orphanages and other special institutions were spread out everywhere, many of them in striking patterns. The people of Boston are so devoted to him that they also give him money to spread schools, churches and all the rest through mission lands around the globe. At the moment, I knew, he was building in his archdiocese a special school for girls that would cost five million dollars, a national seminary for delayed vocations to the priesthood that would cost over two million, a home for retired priests that would cost over a million, a general hospital that would cost eight million. That, I knew, too, was not even the half of it. At the moment, he was doing almost as much in Latin America.

Richard James Cushing was born in South Boston, Massachusetts, on August 24, 1895, the third of five children. His parents had been born in Ireland. He was educated in the Boston public schools and at Boston College High School. After two years at Boston College, he entered St. John's Seminary in Boston. Ordained on May 26, 1921, he served as a parish curate for less than a year and then was appointed assistant to the archdiocesan director of the Society for the Propagation of the Faith. Six years later, he became director. His success in spreading knowledge of the missions throughout the archdiocese was remarkable. In April, 1939, Pope Pius XII named him a monsignor. Two months later he was appointed Titular Bishop of Mela and Auxiliary Bishop of Boston. He was consecrated a bishop on June 29, 1939, by William Cardinal O'Connell, Archbishop of Boston. When the cardinal died, in April, 1944, Bishop Cushing was named administrator. In September, Pope Pius XII named him Archbishop of Boston.

Archbishop Cushing began what is probably the most remarkable building program yet seen in the history of the Church in America. New parishes (eighty-seven at last count, bringing the total well over four hundred), workers' chapels (a dozen of them—at airport, fish pier, shopping and hotel centers), regional high schools (eighteen of them, costing three million each on the average), boarding schools for orphans, mentally deficient and crippled children, new hospitals and additions to existing ones—all this was achieved with a policy of completing payment for each building under construction so that when placed in service it was free from debt.

To help him, and to help them, the archbishop invited over sixty religious orders and congregations to establish or expand foundations in his archdiocese. He encouraged especially those engaged in social and missionary work. The flow of vocations to these groups and to his own archdiocesan priesthood has become well known throughout the world. He had so many vocations that he could institute a "lend-lease" program to provide priests where there was a shortage.

There is no greater friend of the missions than the Archbishop of Boston, no greater beggar ("Useful as a hat is," he says, "its greatest glory is when it serves as a receptacle for alms collected for the poor"), no greater friend of the underdog ("He has a good word for everybody coming down the pike," said one observer of the national scene). He has produced a five-foot shelf of books, pastoral letters and a weekly column in his archdiocesan weekly newspaper, the *Pilot*. He has used every means of communication—radio, TV and photographers' cameras—to be all things to all men all the time. One could sense a mighty cheer reverberating across the country when Pope John XXIII named him a cardinal in November, 1958. He received his red hat at the consistory of December 18, 1958.

As Archbishop of Boston, the cardinal is responsible for nearly 1,700,000 Catholics. It is the largest archdiocese in the country after Chicago. Asthma, ulcers and other troubles have not slowed the cardinal down in caring for this large flock. He is on the go from morning till night, and far into the night—answering letters and looking to his other writing. Much of his work is national in scope. Since 1954, he has been a member of the Administrative Board of the National Catholic Welfare Conference, chairman of the NCWC Youth Department, episcopal moderator of the National Council of Catholic Men and the National Council of Catholic Women, chairman of the Bishops' Committee for Latin America. Whatever he does is news, whether he gives an inaugural prayer in Washington, or helps to raise money to ransom Cuban-invasion prisoners, or dances a jig with the old folks at a Thanksgiving Day party, or puts on a Peruvian

Indian's hat during a visit to priests of his Society of St. James
the Apostle in Latin America.

While I waited to finish my interview with him, a police official told him there was a report that two Cubans had entered
the country to assassinate him for having spoken out against
Cuba's Premier Fidel Castro. The cardinal said: "Well, that
would be an easy way to go." It would be easy for him, but it
would plunge Boston and the country into anguish. He was
not worried. As the following interview shows, he had many
other things on his mind.

QUESTION

*Could you tell us why you left the Council so early, Your
Eminence?*

CARDINAL CUSHING

There were a number of reasons why I stayed only three weeks
at the first session of the Council, but the basic one was simply
that I couldn't understand the Latin that was being spoken.
I have been an administrator all my life, ever since shortly
after ordination to the priesthood, when I was assigned to the
Propagation of the Faith office in Boston. I had never sat
through lectures in Latin of any kind in my life. I can tell
you that I wasn't the only one at the Council who had a
problem with the Latin, but it was especially distressing for
me. The acoustics were fine; the amplifying system was the
most perfect one that I have ever heard anywhere. But such a
variety of accents concealed the words from me! Well, after
a few weeks of sitting through a bewildering barrage of
sound, I was a pretty frustrated man. I began to feel that
there were plenty of experts on the various subjects among
the bishops who could handle anything that would come up.
They didn't need me to help in the work of adjusting stresses
on aspects of Church teaching, understanding previous Council formulations in their setting, and working out what language or terminology to use in order to reach the modern

world. If they were going to go about the task of *aggiorna-mento* in Latin, I might as well be at home, I thought, where so many other things I could do were going undone. All this didn't help my ulcers. So, you see, I really meant it when I proposed that there should be a system of simultaneous translation at the Council, and when I offered to pay for the installation.

QUESTION

Several cardinals I visited in Europe told me they hoped you would return to the Council. "The name of Cushing means so much," they said. If you were to come and rise and state that you wanted something, they said the effect would be most impressive. Would you consider returning to the Council, Your Eminence?

CARDINAL CUSHING

Yes, I have decided to give it another try.

QUESTION

Although you were at the first session only a short time, reports from the non-Catholic delegate-observers indicate that you made a great impression on them.

CARDINAL CUSHING

The intense interest that those men had in the Council was a memorable experience for me. I could see them very well from where I sat, and I noticed that they were working very hard, following everything with the help of interpreters provided by the Secretariat for Promoting Christian Unity. I envied the help in translation that they were getting from Father Gustave Weigel, of Woodstock College in Maryland. I met many of the delegate observers, and on one occasion I invited twenty of them to dinner. Helping the observers was something I decided I could do. I am glad I was able to do something to establish good relations between them and the

Council Fathers. I wanted to do this to help Cardinal Bea and his very important work with the Secretariat for Promoting Christian Unity. I was pleased to notice that Cardinal Bea said in one of his talks at Harvard University that many observations made by the delegate-observers reached beyond the Secretariat and penetrated even into the discussions on the floor of the Council, where they were most useful. In that same talk, Cardinal Bea also quoted Dr. W. A. Visser 't Hooft, general secretary of the World Council of Churches, as saying "the observers are no longer merely observers, since so many contacts and so many conversations have taken place between them and the bishops in the Council."

QUESTION

You made a great contribution to the ecumenical movement when you succeeded in bringing Cardinal Bea to this country for lectures at Harvard University. You must be pleased with the effect of that visit.

CARDINAL CUSHING

I am pleased, and I thank God for taking good care of him on such a long journey. At his age—he is eighty-two, you know —a trip like that is not easy. The idea of having Cardinal Bea speak at Harvard came from Dean Samuel H. Miller of the Harvard Divinity School. The Chauncey Stillman chair of Catholic studies at Harvard was vacant after Christopher Dawson's return to England, so the dean asked me if I thought the funds might be used this year for some Roman Catholic-Protestant theological conferences. I was sure it could be done. Then he asked if I could get Cardinal Bea to come over for the first of the conferences. He felt that if Cardinal Bea addressed the conference, it would mean success for the whole endeavor. That request certainly shows what an impact the Second Vatican Council has had on the intellectual world.

The work of Cardinal Bea has been appreciated everywhere. When I invited the cardinal to come here, I announced that after his visit to Harvard we would go anywhere to anyone who would accept us. I said we would preach our gospel of love and mutual cooperation, a gospel that respects the rights of conscience of all individuals, whether they be Jews, Catholics, or Protestants. Over a hundred requests came in from colleges and universities. It turned out that we could accept only a few, because we did not want to tax the cardinal's strength. The cardinal accepted what he prudently could. His three talks at Harvard were excellent, and very important.

The amazing cardinal—that's what I call him. With all the traveling he did—and all the preparation that went into the talks at Boston College, Harvard, the agape in New York, the sermon in Baltimore, the address at the Catholic University in Washington—he was nevertheless always smiling, always on the go, so simple, so clear, so profound. Father Bernard Leeming calls him a "divine find," and I agree. This great biblical scholar, since he was made a cardinal and president of the Secretariat for Promoting Christian Unity, has probed deeply into the theology of the Mystical Body, right to its New Testament foundations. He has drawn Catholic and Protestant alike to the luminous truths he has unveiled for us with new brilliance.

Fortunately, a collection of Cardinal Bea's articles and addresses, edited by Father Leeming, has been prepared in English, with the title *The Unity of Christians* (Herder and Herder). As you can see from these page proofs, it contains an excellent exposition of the ideas I have just mentioned. I have just persuaded the publishers to put out a paperback edition, and I have ordered ten thousand copies for myself. I intend to distribute these copies gratis where they will be appreciated for the important ideas they contain. I shall give some to the dean of the Harvard Divinity School, others to the Newman Club chaplains at all the colleges in this area, still others to all the Protestant groups that have invited me to speak on the Ecumenical Council.

QUESTION

In his first talk in this country, at Boston College where he was awarded an honorary degree of Doctor of Civil and Canon Law, Cardinal Bea urged practical cooperation in the unity movement on the part of students, and at Harvard he outlined how the academic community could help. How do you think practical cooperation could be achieved in parishes, schools and homes?

CARDINAL CUSHING

We have to begin cultivating the ecumenical attitude right with the little children, by teaching them to pray for all the other children of God as well as Catholics, and to love and respect them. Children who can understand baptism can also understand something about the relationship which baptism establishes among all the baptized. They can grasp something of the truth that all the baptized form a unique family of God, which should be trying to achieve a family unity. They can certainly appreciate the scene where our Lord prays "that all may be one."

The ecumenical attitude depends upon an understanding of the New Testament teaching about baptism and its consequences; the New Testament teaching about the unity between the Father and the Son in the Blessed Trinity; the New Testament teaching about the unity between Christ and His disciples. We need good courses in the New Testament, therefore, especially in our high schools. We must make sure that all the rich teaching of the New Testament about the Mystical Body of Christ is conveyed to our young people.

We have been talking about what we should put into the books our young people use in school. Let me say a word about taking something out, if it is there in any of the books they use. I am thinking about the charge which is sometimes made, that Catholic catechisms or religion textbooks here and there contain material that can sow the seeds of anti-Semitism.

There shouldn't be any anti-Semitism in a Catholic book. Anti-Semitism is not only a violation of God's law of love, it is a falsification of the New Testament record. The Catholic Church does not teach that the Jewish people were cursed by God when their leaders rejected Christ the Messiah. The Catholic Church does not teach that the Jews are a deicide people because they put the Son of God to death on a cross. What the Church does teach is that all mankind—Catholics included—put the Son of God to death on a cross, because it was the sins of all of us that brought Him down to this earth and turned Him toward the cross and put Him up on that cross. No one can despise the Jews for the death of Christ if he has his theology straight; if he wants to despise somebody for the death of Christ, he ought to despise the whole human race. When the Jewish leaders in Jerusalem handed Jesus over to the Romans for execution, they were only our agents in an action for which we are all responsible.

I notice that Cardinal Liénart, in his interview, has a strong statement on this subject—a very good one—and that he quotes St. Peter's sermon where our first Pope tells the Jews he knows they acted in ignorance and that through them God was fulfilling what He had announced beforehand. I might add that if one wants to despise somebody for the death of Christ, he may have to end up despising God Himself, for it was God who sent His Son on this mission of suffering and death. Good Pope John XXIII has taken out of the liturgy some expressions that may well have misled some not too intelligent Christians into anti-Semitic feelings. If there are any sentences in catechisms or religion textbooks along those lines, they had better come out fast, too.

To get back to the question of Christian unity, and how we can develop the ecumenical attitude in our young people, I would like to say that Cardinal Bea made a good point when he said that Catholics take if for granted they should pray and sacrifice for the advancement of the work of the foreign missions (which means working for conversion of non-Christians), and this is as it should be, but, since those who have been baptized are much closer to us than non-Christians, even if they are separated from the See of Peter, we should all take it for granted that we ought to pray and sacrifice for the advancement of the work of Christian unity.

You may remember that, in connection with this idea, in my pastoral letter, "The Call of the Council" (Lent, 1962), I stressed that the laity, along with the members of the hierarchy, are *co-responsible* for the Church. Every Christian labors for his own salvation, but he must also perform with Christ a work of collaboration in dispensing the graces of redemption. Christ prays for unity. So, then, not only priests, but people, too, pray for unity. Christ sacrificed for unity. So, too, priests, people—children, too—sacrifice for unity.

We have passed through a period of history when religious controversies forced us to put special emphasis on the dignity of the teaching and ruling authorities in the Church. There built up among the people, as a result, a tendency to look upon the Church as something outside themselves, as an authority to which they are subject. But we have emerged into a period of fuller appreciation of the doctrine of the Mystical Body of Christ and the doctrine of the Eucharist. Now we see more clearly that the Church is a living body in which the laity share full membership, for they share in the entire life of that body. The people are "the holy people." They share in the life of Christ; they are the active participants in the worship offered by the Church to the Father; they should be active participants in the work of the Church whether that is for the missions, for the perfection of Catholics (in the Christian Family Movement, Cana Conferences, etc.), or for Christian unity. We must prepare our young people for this broad range that their future activity should have.

They should know, therefore, that union can come only through grace, and they must pray for that grace; the search for what Christ wished for His Church should be unbiased, and that means an unbiased study of Scripture and the Fathers of the Church; the spirit of their activity should be open-minded, which means that they should recognize good wherever they find it and should cooperate with good people where there is no compromise in matters of faith.

I have said this before, but I will say it again, because it is a good example of the open-minded spirit I have just referred to: there are no Protestant slums; there is no Roman Catholic juvenile delinquency; there is no Jewish civic pessimism. These problems of slums, delinquency and corruption that confront the American community push out far beyond sectarian boundaries. Just as the frontiers of the Church pass through each member of the Church, so the stains of these problems pass through all the elements of our pluralistic society. To put this positively, I like what the Episcopal Bishop of Massachusetts said on Washington's Birthday last year, when he was speaking about charges of "corruption" in Massachusetts: "Here is a chance for practical church unity. There are fellow Christians, Protestants and Roman Catholics in your communities concerned with these things. Work with them. Our Jewish brothers have been inspired by the same God of justice whom we worship. Let us work together. Let the forces of religion together face the needs of public morality in government and business alike." I say Amen to that.

Participation in what is called the ecumenical dialogue calls for special training, but, thanks to our Catholic colleges and universities, that special training is no longer found only among the clergy. We have a number of Catholic graduates now who got enough out of their college theology courses, because they really dug into them, that they can take a hand in the dialogue with some confidence. When Cardinal Bea spoke at Harvard and said we must first work out what we have in common with our separated brethren, his words were carried by radio all over my archdiocese, and I know that in the parishes there were men and women who could follow him quite well. They knew what he was talking about when he said that exact discovery of the Christian goods we have in common is a help in distinguishing clearly the differences between ourselves and our separated brethren. These people I refer to can understand Pope John when he says he prefers to emphasize what tends to unite men and to accompany every man as far along his way as he can without betraying the demands of justice and truth. These men and women know a lot more about the truth, the teaching of the Church and justice than their parents did. The sacrifices their parents made for them, that they might have a complete Catholic education, have produced this fruitful harvest of well-educated laity that the Church now enjoys in this country. These men and women know enough about the faith to handle themselves in cooperative interracial work, social action and dialogues. That is why, when I went to address the national convention of the National Council of Catholic Nurses last year, I put the question: "Why weren't Protestant nurses invited to attend?" I said then that the whole idea of Catholic councils for professional people, youngsters, laymen and laywomen needed modernization. I meant that we not only do not want to live in a ghetto, but we have an obligation either to "get out there" and bring the good of our faith with us, or to "bring them in," in order to share it with them.

QUESTION

You have certainly backed up those statements by your own engagement in the dialogue, Your Eminence. I am thinking, for example, of your TV discussion with a Protestant Episcopal bishop and the program on which you answered telephone calls from the listening audience at large.

CARDINAL CUSHING

I know that nothing like this has happened around here before, but I have been invited to talk at Protestant churches and I intend to accept those engagements that I can work into my schedule. For years, now, I have approved and encouraged the growth of the ecumenical spirit among my priests. Protestant clergymen and Orthodox leaders have been engaged in serious theological conversations with priests of my archdiocese. I have approved and endorsed these meetings in the hope that this is one of the best ways to foster the understanding and charity that are needed for ultimate union.

From those meetings, and from my own conversations with Protestants and Orthodox, I know there are definite areas of theological divergence, but I know, too, that many of our hostilities of the past have been due to misunderstandings. I often encounter questions that show ignorance of what the Church really teaches. Sometimes, when they know the essential point the Church teaches (for example, on matters like divorce, birth control, etc.), non-Catholics lack the knowledge of our faith that is needed to have the problem in proper focus. We do them a great service when we help them to achieve the proper focus, and they understand us better. It works both ways. Our understanding them better reduces friction to a minimum. We keep our convictions, but we get rid of the prejudices which make the idea of Christian unity impossible. Then there is a chance for the reestablishing of the historic truth.

The exchange of views between priests and ministers has proceeded with a spirit of fraternal charity. I think we are establishing a favorable climate for Christian unity, through prayer, mutual respect and love for one another. We are growing in respect for the action of Christ and His Holy Spirit, wherever we find it. I was so impressed by the fervor of the Protestant ecumenical group known as the Brothers of Taizé that I approved establishment of one of their centers in my archdiocese, and it now has another branch here. Seminary professors and other priests have participated in discussions at these houses, and some of our more competent laity are now coming along in unity work. Now I am going to get into it myself in a bigger way by speaking before Protestant congregations.

In all the work I have described, as well as in the speaking I intend to do, we are not trying to make converts. We are not yet at the stage of discussing practical means of union. We are just trying to understand each other. We are just trying to explain as clearly as we can exactly what we believe, what we teach. We are not heading into indifferentism or compromise or surrender or anything like that. On the other hand, we are not attacking the assertions of other faiths. In other words, we are doing just what Pope John has asked the Second Vatican Council to do when he said in his sermon opening the Council: "The Catholic Church, raising the torch of religious truth by means of this Ecumenical Council, desires to show herself to be the loving mother of all, benign, patient, full of mercy and goodness toward the children separated from her. . . ." And he also said: "She considers that she meets the needs of the present day by demonstrating the validity of her teaching rather than by condemnation."

QUESTION

It is well known that you have many friends among the Orthodox Christians, those not in union with the Holy See. I know that some of them hope you can help to build a bridge between East and West, that is, between the churches of East and West.

CARDINAL CUSHING

I have been asked to deliver an address at the close of the Boston College Theological Conference, one of the events marking the centennial of the college, which has become an important university. I shall take that occasion to speak on this very question. I intend to recall these words of our Lord: "If thou art offering thy gift at the altar, and there rememberest that thy brother has anything against thee, leave thy gift before the altar and go first be reconciled to thy brother, and then come and offer thy gift." In those words I take it that our Lord assigns the priorities in our service and in our sacrifices for Him. We are first to be reconciled to our brothers. "That they may be one" is the design of our Redeemer which we must bring to realization. It is a serious obligation, not a secondary matter, and not something only for specialists. It is something entrusted to the conscience of each individual. I shall ask, then: "If your brother has anything against you . . ." and I shall ask: "Have our Orthodox brethren anything against us?"

Now, one may have to make many allowances for the complications of history, but in simple honesty we have to confess that our Orthodox brethren may hold certain things against us. I am thinking, for example, of neglect in the matter of helping them when they were attacked by Moslems. I am thinking of pride and ruthlessness on the part of the Crusaders—just think of the sack of Constantinople—and the assumption so often encountered in the history of our relations that Latin customs and outlooks were superior. Look at the controversial and hostile spirit of so much writing in the West about the Orthodox, even in comparatively recent times; the attempts of not a few "missionaries" to Latinize the whole Church; the very language we often use about union, that the Orthodox must be "led back," must "submit," must "return to obedience." These are things that our brethren have against us, and perhaps there are more. I say, therefore, that we should approach them to ask forgiveness, and to ask that they come with us that we may lay our gifts upon God's altar together.

The unity willed by Christ and sought by the Church is not an absorption, not a Latinization, not a diminution. On the contrary, it is an enrichment, a reevaluation, a new radiance, the beginning of a new era. I intend to quote Pope Pius XII to back up these points:

It is necessary that all peoples of the Oriental rites, in everything that concerns their particular history, genius and character, should enjoy legitimate liberty, insofar as there is nothing contrary to the true and integral doctrine of Jesus Christ. This should be known and given the most studious attention, and as much by those who were born in the bosom of the Church as by those who in longing and desire tend toward it. All must be convinced that in no way will they be put under pressure to change their own proper and lawful rites, or their ancient traditions and institutions, for Latin institutions or rites. Each and all of these rites must be held in equal honor and esteem, because they form within the one Church, their common Mother, a royal entourage of truth. What is more, diversity of rites and institutions keeps intact all that is ancient and precious in each church, and adds luster to the truth and essential unity.

You see, I hold that our whole approach toward our Orthodox brethren must be inspired by honest acknowledgment of our faults and deficiencies; by sincere humility, admiration and gratitude; by patience and by charity; by grasping every possible opportunity for cooperation and for dialogue. That is why I will beg our Orthodox brethren to regard the Eastern rites united with the Holy See not as deserters from their cause, but as ambassadors carrying the traditions and the institutions of the East into the inner councils of the West. I hope the Orthodox will allow that the Eastern rites united with the Holy See have a unique vocation to bring to us the insights and the traditions of the East.

I know that some of our Eastern rites have complaints against their present status. Patriarch Maximos IV and the Greek Melchite hierarchy have complained that the Oriental patriarchs are ranked below cardinals, an arrangement which, they say, fails to recognize the traditional setup of the Church; that converts in the East are allowed to choose either the Oriental or the Latin Rite, but in the West they are allowed only into the Latin Rite, which, they say, is an attempt to suffocate the Oriental rites; that the Roman Curia wants a Latin Patriarch of Jerusalem, which would be an insult to the Orientals. I must admit that I am unable to make any judgment about the justice of these and other complaints, but I will say that complaints of this kind must be settled before we can hope to build a lasting bridge between the East and the West. They probably will be settled before the end of the Second Vatican Council.

I will make these practical suggestions, too, that we should develop a greater interest in the history of the divided churches, and that we should make accessible to a greater number of people both inside and outside the Orthodox and Catholic Churches the thought and the writings of the great Fathers—I mean translations of Oriental works into English and of Western works into Russian and modern Greek. There is some of this work in production; we need much more. In fact, I will put it this way: We hear much today about biblical theology. But can any theology be truly biblical if it is not also truly patristic? Can we understand the word of God in the Bible unless we also understand it in the Christian tradition? Return to the Bible must carry with it return to the Fathers, and this is a truth that our Orthodox brethren can teach us today.

QUESTION

I asked Cardinal Koenig and Cardinal Alfrink if they thought a common Bible for all English-speaking Christians using a common language was a real possibility. They agreed that it was, although Cardinal Alfrink added there were great difficulties to be overcome. Do you endorse the idea, Your Eminence?

CARDINAL CUSHING

Yes, from what I know about it I would say that a common translation in English, to be used by both Catholics and Protestants, is possible. Cardinal Koenig has a background of biblical studies, and Cardinal Alfrink was a professor of Sacred Scripture for many years. What they say about the idea, therefore, is especially significant. They can say with more assurance than I can that Catholic and Protestant scholars use the same Hebrew and Greek manuscripts of the Bible, and that their work is so objective today that they often can arrive at the same translation for the same phrase or sentence. Cardinal Alfrink brings up the difficulty of having to choose between traditional translations for certain terms. He told you that in Dutch the Protestants have one word for "temptation" and the Catholics another. I suppose we would have the same problem when it came to choosing between "justice" and "righteousness." He said he couldn't see any compromise; the solution would have to be that one side would give up its word and adopt the other. Well, it might take some time before that kind of thing could be worked out here, but I can certainly say this: when the time comes for working out a common translation that would be acceptable to both Catholics and Protestants, I will hope for its success, because it would be a tremendous help in the cause of Christian unity. The Bible means everything to Protestants, and one of the most encouraging things to them has been the great upsurge of biblical interest among Catholics. Our renewal of respect for the Bible, the return to the Bible for theological terminology, the focus on Scripture for our sermons and our teaching of catechism has heartened them, just as it has strengthened and enriched us.

QUESTION

As an archbishop, you are constantly involved, more than most members of the Church, in the complexities of Church law. Do you foresee changes in that law by Council decisions?

CARDINAL CUSHING

Yes. If the Council is faithful to the pastoral approach that has been established, and which Pope John himself requested, there should be considerable changes in Church law. After all, Canon Law is the result of pastoral needs. But the needs of one time are not the needs of another. The laws of the past that were put on the books to take care of problems of the past may not be of much help to a later generation. In fact, they can sometimes be a hindrance in the care of souls. That is why I think the Council can, and should, do something about our many problems in the handling of mixed marriages.

As it is now, the requirement that a non-Catholic partner make the famous promises before marriage is an irritant to many, and some, it is clear from what happens subsequently, make the promises in bad faith. If we no longer required the promises, we would not be revoking any divine law; we would not be changing any dogma of the Church. There are good reasons for considering such a move. Remember when mixed marriages could not be performed in church but had to take place in the rectory? We changed that and permitted the use of the church. Instead of separating that ceremony from a holy environment, we now start those marriages off in a context of church, which opens up the possibility of many actual graces being given instead of the generating of feelings of frustration, hostility, etc.

Many people forget that it was only half a century ago that we had changes in the Church's marriage legislation. We made changes then, and the Church went on. I must say, though, that it would be a good thing if the Council revised that particular legislation, which concerned the form of consent. Cases about defect of form have piled up as a result. We could use something to break the logjam. It would help, too, if diocesan and archdiocesan marriage tribunals could have the power to settle a number of the cases that now have to go to Rome, which means a lot of work and a lot of delay.

There is another big logjam in connection with the Index of Prohibited Books. You know what a great number of schools, colleges and universities we have in the Boston area. It is simply impossible to handle all the requests that would come in on a personal basis, for permission to read books on the Index that teachers think their students should know something about. I have added to the problem myself, in a sense, by recommending and approving courses on Communism in high schools. As I have said before, there is no shortcut to studying the Communist method of disseminating the Communist line except by continual examination of the official Red publications. A competent instructor will always be required to know the subject he is handling from primary sources; he will have to go over them critically and untangle the language plays in those publications; he will have to cultivate an equally critical attitude in his pupils. If the course is going to succeed, the instructor has to see some of the Communist propaganda, to give his students the "accurate and complete information on the activity of the enemy" that Pope John has spoken about in addressing the Catholic press, but which he undoubtedly meant for all educated Catholic lay readers.

When the bishops of the world were asked to submit their ideas for the coming Second Vatican Council, I was one of those who recommended abolishing the present Index and the procedure connected with it. I thought it should be "phased out" in view of the pastoral realities facing us. I was glad to learn that Cardinal Ottaviani, who, as secretary of the Holy Office, has charge of the Index, recently agreed it would be a good idea for the Council Fathers to "examine the problem of the Index in the context of the present day." The interview with Cardinal Ottaviani, published in *Civiltà Cattolica,* quoted him as saying that an effective solution of the problem should also include the other instruments of social communication: films, radio and television. I think we have worked out a very sensible arrangement with regard to Catholic opinion about movies in the United States, through the new approach to classifications made by the Legion of Decency. I think we American bishops could offer the Council some good, practical advice as a result of our experiences in this country, and I certainly look forward to the pastoral benefits that will accrue to the Church as a result.

In all of this discussion about reforming Canon Law, I would like to say something I said in my pastoral letter on the Council about reform in the Church in general: the important thing to remember with regard to reform is that it is done within the Church, within the framework of ecclesiastical authority, within the visible Body—it is the work of the Spirit sanctifying the Body. When it takes place outside this framework, it is not reform but a wounding action on the Body of Christ, and so opposed to the work of the Spirit, no matter how lofty its motives.

QUESTION

In your pastoral letter on the Council, you said: "Within the local parish there also is need of change." What did you have in mind?

CARDINAL CUSHING

To some extent I had in mind that we need changes in present Canon Law about pastors, parishes, etc. Here is just a little example. The way Church law is now, if someone appeals to me for permission to call the church just over the parish border theirs, I can't give that permission. With our modern society in such a mobile state, bishops ought to be able to do a number of things the law doesn't now permit them to do. The so-called exodus to suburbia, urban development, trailer camps, vacation resorts mushrooming, etc., create situations that Church law as it is now didn't envision. Furthermore, we have a great variety of parish organizations that were effective last century, but I think we ought to question whether they are still effective. If they have lost the Christian dynamic that once gave them purpose, then I say we need a change. It is not a question of change just for the sake of change; it is a matter of meeting modern pastoral needs.

I think every parish should come up with its solution to the geriatric problem, and I think every parish should do something about its retarded children. Old people and defective children should not have to be shipped off to remote institutions if they can be cared for locally. If a wing can be added to the parish plant for old folks, with rooms or little apartments, and if something similar can be done for handicapped children, these people remain in a normal, healthy parish environment; they are still part of their own neighborhood. Also, the people of the parish become involved in spiritual and corporal works of mercy that they should be responsible for, along with the pastor and the bishop. This is the kind of thing I have in mind when I say that this Council has to get right down to the grass roots. We must do more than talk about the nature of the Mystical Body, more than state the fact that we are all members of that Body and should be active members. We should indicate to the laity the areas in which they must take special concern, and we should set up parish life in the future so that everybody gets into the work of the Mystical Body as well as its life. As I said before, the laity, along with the members of the hierarchy, are co-responsible for the Church. If they have their share of the Church's works in their own parish, they will appreciate this truth.

As you know already, I plan to bring the laity into the synod that I will convoke in Boston sometime after the close of the Council. They will have a voice in preparations for the synod and in the establishing of regulations for the archdiocese that will be drawn up in accordance with the decrees and the spirit of the Second Vatican Council.

QUESTION

You have done a number of things with regard to priests that indicate you have a broader view of a priest's work than many other bishops. Would you tell us something about that?

CARDINAL CUSHING

You refer, no doubt, to my encouragement of missionary experience for diocesan priests. I think, frankly, that the idea of missionary orders or congregations as solely responsible for the propagation of the faith is a thing of the past. I encourage diocesan priests to consider spending a few years on a missionary assignment—at home or abroad—in such a way that they do not lose any seniority status for promotions in their home diocese. I founded the Society of St. James the Apostle for this purpose, and it has attracted priests from dioceses and countries far beyond the borders of Boston.

There are many advantages of this program, but one I like especially is the way it spreads missionary consciousness throughout the Church. Our Church is a mission Church, but if priests spend their whole lives in their home diocese, they may not have the full appreciation of that concept. When priests come back after a few years in a foreign country, or in less Catholic parts of our own country, they have a real rather than a notional knowledge of the mission apostolate, and they can communicate it to their people. Imagine what that can mean—to take just one practical point—in support of the missions. The American people send many millions of dollars annually to Rome for distribution throughout the mission world, but the amount could be tripled if the people had a more proximate awareness of the need for their support.

Just watch the increase in vocations, too, as a result of priests having this missionary experience. Our young people's spirit of generosity would be immensely stimulated if they understood that they could have some years on the missions after they entered the diocesan priesthood—that it was not work reserved only to religious orders and congregations. This sharing of priests with mission areas has, of course, a number of benefits for the mission areas, especially in the cultivation of vocations. The presence of a priest where there might otherwise never be a priest and the good example he gives provide the occasion of many graces to young people, and people not so young. I have seen that happen often with regard to chaplains in the military services. Areas of the Church that don't provide many chaplains miss out on what I have seen happen. I have allowed many of my priests to spend a few years in the military, and I have seen a good flow of vocations from the soldiers and sailors around them. We owe it to the draftees, just as we owed it to our fighting men during the wars, to give them spiritual help, but when we do, we get a return in spiritual benefits. Here is an example of what can happen. I had a request for a priest to help solve a situation on an island off the Alaska coast. There were three nuns and eighty-five people there without a priest, but something could be worked out if another priest were added to the Fairbanks area. A United States marine captain who had become a priest volunteered for the assignment. See what I mean?

QUESTION

I know that Cardinal Suenens sent you a copy of his book The Nun in the World. *What do you think of his proposal that Sisters should become spiritual directors of women?*

CARDINAL CUSHING

I read Cardinal Suenens' book, and I agree with him that the role of the Sisters in the parish should be greatly increased. They should be engaged in social work; they should help the visiting nurses in homes; and they should share the fruits of their spiritual life with the people around them. Not every Sister will have the talent or ability to be a spiritual guide for other women, but those who are so gifted should be given every opportunity to make the most of their gifts. In addition to guidance in spiritual matters, there are so many special cases I know about where the help and guidance of a Sister would be the solution to a situation that now goes without any answer. Take, for example, the case of a teen-age girl who has had a breakdown, physical or moral. You wouldn't want to put her in an institution, but she needs help. If we could put a Sister on her case, we could leave the girl right in her home, her neighborhood, her parish. There are all kinds of possibilities in opening up this whole field to Sisters.

In the interview he gave you, Cardinal Suenens also says that training in social awareness should be built into all the years of the priest's seminary course, and something like that should be done in the formation of Sisters. I would like to add that awareness of the Church's mission aspect should be built into the whole course of training, too, just as development of the ecumenical attitude should be. All of these attitudes should be built right into parish life and right into our whole school system, from the earliest grades all the way up.

We have concentrated for a long time on the approach through the schools. That is chiefly how we have counted on reaching the people both at home and abroad in mission lands. I am thinking more and more that we should perhaps concentrate on the approach through social action. I am very much impressed by the missionaries who come into a village and set up some industry that puts the place on its feet economically. We've gotten certain results by moving in and setting up a school, but setting up an industry can perhaps be more effective. When you have elevated the economic status of the people, they are in a position to do something for others, instead of always being on the receiving end. They can go right into the social apostolate, and they can support mission endeavors. They can set up their geriatric centers and homes for children and do the work of Christ for the less-favored members of the Mystical Body.

QUESTION

For some time, I know, you had doubts about the movement for more vernacular in the liturgy, specifically in the Mass. How do you feel now about this?

CARDINAL CUSHING

When I think of priests in mission areas, trying to communicate the faith to people who do not have a tradition of Latin in the liturgy or even as a subject in school, I must admit that the vernacular in the first part of the Mass would help a great deal, for that is the part of the Mass where the people profess their faith and are further instructed. In our environment of more developed tradition, where the use of hand missals is so common, the Latin liturgy is, to me, a very beautiful and reasonable thing, and I have often thought what a bond of unity it is in various countries. I sometimes celebrate Mass at St. Coletta's School for Exceptional Children. You should hear those children give the responses in a dialogue Mass. They answer in Latin better than so-called normal children, but, of course, although it is beautiful to me, they don't understand what they are saying. My thoughts go out over the parishes. How many other people really do not understand what they are saying in giving the Latin responses? I have been won over to the side of those who see great pastoral benefits from putting more vernacular in the liturgy. I now favor having at least the whole first part of the Mass in the vernacular. Furthermore, I very much want to have the priest's daily Divine Office in the vernacular, or at least that an option be given to the priest, so that he may recite it in Latin or in the vernacular. It is a pity that so many priests read their Latin prayers for an hour every day and understand so little of the spiritual riches in the Psalms for the day and in the commentaries of the Fathers of the Church.

QUESTION

It is rumored that the American bishops will present a statement or statements on the Church-State question at the coming session of the Council. Do you plan to speak on the matter?

CARDINAL CUSHING

Obviously, the whole Church-State subject is of great interest to the American bishops. If I can be of help to the Council in this matter, I will take whatever opportunity arises. I certainly think it would be helpful that the Council know how satisfied the American bishops are and have been with our United States Constitution and its clear prohibition that any authority or power be exercised in religious matters by either Federal or State government. It could be pointed out to the Council that this constitutional prohibition was not intended by the makers of the Constitution as a denial or suppression of religion but as a defense and protection of it. We have had to insist upon this at various times in this country, even to the extent of reminding the Supreme Court that it has said repeatedly in its statements that "we are a religious people." Once we get the present Court straightened out and back on the right track we can point again with pride to the fact that religion flourishes in this country; the Church is exempt from taxation; prayers are said in the Congress; chaplains serve in war and peace; our priests and seminarians are exempt from military service. The social obligation of worshiping God is acknowledged. We have religious liberty, and it is a good thing.

There should not be any denial of religious liberty in the political and social order. I certainly would not want anything done by the Council that would give the impression that Catholic doctrine demands full religious liberty for Catholics where they constitute a minority but denies it to others when Catholics constitute a majority. We should stress that nobody is to come to the faith except voluntarily, because faith is a free gift of God. We do not want the authority of the state coming in to defend the Church against other religious confessions. It's too dangerous, even if it were possible, but, more importantly, we must respect personal conscience and the dignity of every man created in God's image—therefore free. All of this means that there should be full religious liberty in the political order.

There is a lot more that could be said about relations between Church and State. For example, it is in the nature of things that the state should respect the Church, and not only the Catholic Church but all manifestations of religion. If the Holy Spirit is acting in other churches (and that is certainly evident at least in movements for Christian unity), then you have another argument for religious liberty. Perhaps it would be wise to have several American bishops present speeches on the subject, in order that its various aspects could be covered more adequately. There is nothing in Council procedure that would prohibit such a presentation spread out over several speeches by different speakers. If I can get somebody to put a text into Latin for me, I will do my share of the job. At any rate, I am sure that the experience of the Church in the United States is destined in the providence of God to make its contribution in the deliberations of the Second Vatican Council for the best formulation of the Christian principles that should govern the relations between Church and State. I am sure that anything we have to say will be studied with profound respect by the Council Fathers.

Cardinal Cushing has organized many things in his lifetime. Bostonians know well his Sen Fu Club for women and Father Jim Hennessey Club for men—both organized to spread knowledge of the missions throughout homes and parish organizations; his St. Francis Refuge, caring for seven hundred men a day on Boston's "skid row"; his network of leagues and guilds, making up the Cardinal Cushing Charity Fund—usually, in each case, people of one profession or occupation working to support a project they would naturally be interested in; the ecumenical center in Boston (Cardinal Cushing Institute for Religious Understanding) to be staffed by the Paulist Fathers.

Nearest to the cardinal's heart, however, is the Society of St. James the Apostle, organized in July, 1958. Late in the summer of 1962, he revealed that he would like to join the society: "I would gladly resign my office here and work for my confreres in Peru, Ecuador, Bolivia and other countries where they will be assigned in the future." It would be wonderful, he said, "in the closing years to be part of the missionary effort of the Church for which I worked so long behind a desk or traveled from parish to parish preaching the missionaries' needs." He had, in fact, asked the Holy See two years earlier for permission to become a missionary, but he had been persuaded to remain in Boston. There is something else he long ago decided he wanted—to be buried at St. Coletta's, the school he founded for the children he calls "exceptional." By their prayers, the people of Boston and many other places through the world have so far frustrated the fulfillment of both desires. They want him to keep on for many more years fulfilling his episcopal motto: *Ut Cognoscant Te* ("That they may know Thee").

✌ Postscript ঌ

"This is something that should be published, but do not attribute it to me." It was a cardinal speaking. He continued: "Why do I not want this comment attributed to me? Am I afraid? No, I am not afraid of anything or anybody." He explained that his role in the Council, as he had discerned it evolving, was to be a conciliator between opposing groups. It would hurt this important role, he felt, if his name were connected with a criticism like the one he had just given. He had just complained about the influence of "so-called experts who deliver lectures in Rome during the Council under the auspices of one or another bishop." Some of the bishops who attend these lectures, the cardinal said, are "so enthralled by the dynamic presentation of the speaker or by ideas they had not given much thought to before that, the next thing one knows, these bishops are advancing the ideas in the Council." In other words, he explained, "some bishops are equivalently being used as tools by theologians and scholars outside the ranks of the Council Fathers." This, the cardinal complained, was "in some cases a bad influence." It was then that he said: "This is something that should be published, but do not attribute it to me."

In preparing this book, I visited and talked with twelve cardinals and fourteen bishops. They represented four different continents. In many of these discussions there was no intention of a formal interview for publication. Some who do not appear in the preceding chapters—as well as some who do—gave me ideas and facts which they wanted published, but not by attribution to them. The reasons they gave in each case convinced me that it would be proper to withhold their names. I shall give those reasons in each case. Under the heading of "another Council Father," therefore, I have gathered what several asked me to include in this book.

The cardinal who complained about "so-called experts" and their lectures obviously was not referring to all of the theologians who gave lectures during the days of the Council. Other cardinals and bishops had high praise for lectures they had attended. Some of the prelates admitted they had been so busy up to the moment of departure for Rome that they had studied little or nothing of the *schemata*. They were particularly grateful for lectures that brought them up to date on current problems in the Church. "How can a busy bishop catch up in any better way than by listening to an expert sum up the developments in his field?" one bishop said to me.

The cardinal who criticized certain theologians' lectures also had some harsh things to say about pamphlets and brochures that were circulated among the Council Fathers during the first session of the Council. In this he was rather generally backed up by other bishops, who were irritated by one or another publication that had been distributed to them by interested parties. One large publication (over six hundred pages, handsomely printed, with a glossy paperback cover) came in for particularly strong criticism: *Complotto contro la Chiesa,* by Maurice Pinay.

One of the mysteries of the Council to this day is: who financed the printing of this large volume, which was distributed to all the Council Fathers? Another mystery is the identity of the author. The name sounds French, but none of the French bishops seemed to know him. The text was in Italian, and the book was printed in Rome. Some thought the author must be an Italian masquerading under a French name. The book (*Conspiracy Against the Church*) charged that, "however incredible it may seem," there is a "fifth column" within the hierarchy of the Church "made up of agents controlled by Freemasonry and Communism and the hidden power that governs these organizations." These agents, the book claimed, were to be found in the ranks of "certain cardinals, archbishops and bishops who form a kind of progressive wing in the Council and who are attempting to make the Council adopt perverse reforms."

The ruin of the Church desired by these "agents" is described in great detail. A major element of the plot is the plan whereby the Church will reverse her teaching on a number of points, for example, in her attitude toward the Jews, "those reprobates, as St. Augustine described them." Such a reversal of attitude on the part of the Church, the plotters hope, will dismay the faithful so much that the Church will lose her influence over them. There are many pages on the false theological ideas that the plotters are attempting to sow, but again and again the question of the Jews comes up till it is quite obvious that the book is the latest in that long line of literature which portrays the Jews as the masterminds of a world conspiracy that is doing the work of the devil.

One cardinal told me that he had not even opened the book. Another said that he had, and he was quite angry. Another Council Father said: "The Council will say nothing about the Jews, but this book is not the reason why."

Apparently, in the cutting down of the *schemata* that the first session had shown was quite necessary if the Council were to be completed within a reasonable time, detailed condemnation of anti-Semitism was eliminated in favor of a general statement that would cover the obligation of fraternal love for all races and nations. Some felt, in fact, that the statement of the Council released on October 20, 1962, had sufficiently taken care of the matter with its declaration: "We proclaim that all men are brothers, irrespective of the race or nation to which they belong." The Pope's encyclical letter, *Pacem in Terris*, would also touch on the racial question along with other matters that the Council would therefore not have to deal with.

Another Council Father gave me some observations on the various proposals for reintroducing the office of deacon in the Church, in the sense that the deacon would be allowed to marry and to remain "what he is, a helper to the priest, commissioned to preach and teach, distribute Holy Communion and be responsible for the corporate charity of the Christian community." The supporters for this idea, the bishop explained, expect it to be the solution for the problem of shortage of priests, especially in countries like the Latin American republics. Many people in German-speaking countries, as well as in France, he told me, have been hoping for the reintroduction of this kind of deacon. He was one of the bishops at the meeting of more than eighty Council Fathers which was held in Munich early in February, 1963. He did not particularly want to be identified with what he was about to tell me, because he did not agree with all of the ideas. He thought they were something the readers of this book should think about, however, and I agreed with him. He certainly must have intended that I should at least identify him as one of the eighty German-speaking bishops meeting in Munich while I was there. The very things that he said showed that much about him.

"With German thoroughness," he said with a smile, "it was suggested that the cultural level of the elementary teacher would be satisfactory for the deacon, while academic status would be necessary for the priest." He deliberately concealed from me whether this "suggestion" came up at a meeting of the bishops or of their theologians, who were present en masse both for the bishops' meetings and for the convention of their theological society which immediately followed the bishops' two-day conference. I was being given this information after the theologians' convention had ended.

"There is an ironical danger to the project," he continued. "It reminds one of the successful *Religionsgespräche* between Catholics and Protestants, a short time after the Reformation, which sometimes were quite successful and ended up with the Catholic turning Protestant and the Protestant turning Catholic." The connection with the idea of the deacons was this: "While Protestants increasingly discover the sacrificial aspect of Holy Communion, Catholics in large parts of the world would be served by deacons holding Communion service."

Then this Council Father told me that one of his theologians held this opinion: the idea to ordain married older men, who have given years of faithful service to the Church as laymen, should not be given up simply on the grounds that Pope John has warned against any attack on the celibate priesthood. There was another element that entered into the case. It was not being suggested that men should enter the seminary as celibates, and be ordained as celibates, with the understanding that they would be free to marry if celibacy should prove to be too much of a burden. The normal priest would still be a celibate, but, the theologian proposed, in countries where there was a dangerous shortage of priests the bishop should be allowed to choose and ordain people older or younger, married or unmarried, with or without academic background, in order to make sure that Mass and the sacraments were available for all Catholics.

The second category of priests, according to this plan, might have to refer difficult cases of conscience in confession to their more learned confreres. Their personal experience of the human problems of their flock, it was argued, would amply make up for the comparative lack of religious culture.

It was argued, too, that the existence of this second category of priests would make it possible to raise the intellectual level of theological studies. Instead of merely having a textbook knowledge, the celibate priests would study theology thoroughly before being ordained, "and they would continue their studies after ordination, in order to be able to give not only milk to the babies but also solid food to the grown-ups."

When I discussed these ideas with another Council Father, he frowned and pursed his lips. He said: "But that would make two classes of priests . . ." and his voice trailed off in doubtful silence. There was one other point that was mentioned incidentally in all of this proposal. Where the other bishop explained that his theologian was not suggesting that the clergy would start as celibate but have an option to marry if celibacy proved too much of a burden, he added: "even though it may be hoped that 'lapsed' married priests might find it easier in the future to have their marriage regularized." Now this other Council Father took up that point. The frown vanished from his forehead. "That," he said, "we must do something about; there are so many shepherds in the mist everywhere. We must do something to bring them back to the sacraments . . . " and his voice trailed off into pensive silence.

Another Council Father said to me: "Do you wonder what is going on, with the Holy Father accepting the Balzan Peace Prize and then receiving the daughter and the son-in-law of the Soviet Premier?" I suspected he had heard some Catholics wondering out loud (as I had heard some) whether the Holy Father fully appreciated what he was getting into in dealing with a man like Premier Khrushchev. There were rumors that an encyclical letter was coming which would set the stage for a visit by Premier Khrushchev to Pope John, and that the visit could lead to the setting up of at least limited diplomatic relations. Some observers thought the Soviets were simply making a play for votes in Italy's coming elections. Others feared it was propaganda that the Soviets would aim at Catholic populations in Western Europe and Latin America. The timing suggested to other observers that Khrushchev had good reasons to seek better relations with the West. They connected developments with Khrushchev's troubles in Moscow (Stalinists in the Kremlin) and in Peiping (hard-line Chinese Communists). They thought Khrushchev was figuring that easing of Church tensions in satellite countries would help him hold the support of the leaders in those countries.

"No," said the Council Father, "all these calculations miss the mark. I will tell you what is going on, but I do not want you to say who it was that gave you this information." He then explained why he wanted to remain anonymous: "You see, I have this information from the best possible source, and it

would not be proper for me to give it out in my name." I took
it that he was referring to Pope John himself, and I wondered
how I could possibly put the item in the book. "Oh, that is
all right," said the Council Father. "You see, there are many
who have been told." It was, indeed, something that should be
told, I agreed.

"Instead of looking at all the places you have mentioned,"
he continued, "Italy, Moscow, Peiping, etc, you should go back
to the Cuban crisis. You remember how it seemed then that we
were poised at the brink of a nuclear holocaust? How we wondered whether Mr. Kennedy or Mr. Khrushchev would push
the button that would let loose the missiles and rockets with
their atomic warheads?"

I remembered the crisis well. I had never felt such a chilling
fear sweep across the country as we had experienced in the
United States that dread day when Mr. Kennedy was waiting
for an answer from Mr. Khrushchev by six o'clock. The news
of the Pearl Harbor disaster had not been as chilling as the wait
of that day at the height of the Cuban crisis. The one was news
after the event, as most pieces of news are; this one had been
news of impending holocaust.

"Thanks to the speed of modern communications, the Holy
Father knew how desperate the situation was, in Moscow and
in Washington. And, thanks to those same communications,
the world's leaders simultaneously received the impact of Pope
John's message calling for peace. You remember that address?
The one that some thought was 'tainted' with neutralism? Those
words touched the hearts of Khrushchev, Kennedy and many
others."

"As I understand it," the Council Father continued, "Premier
Khrushchev said something like: 'This is just what the situation
needs; we must draw back from the nuclear holocaust.' He
wanted to communicate with the Holy Father, but he was advised that he could scarcely expect to do that while he still held
in prison the head of a whole Christian Church. 'Who is that?'
asked Premier Khrushchev. 'Archbishop Slipyi,' was the reply.

'I do not even know if the man is alive,' said the Premier, but he gave the order: 'Find him and bring him here.' That was how Archbishop Slipyi came to be released, and that was how one thing led to another.

"'The Holy Father regards it as a providential act of God that his words reached the hearts they did, and that they brought the world back from the brink of disaster," said the Council Father. It was not the Pope alone who spoke to the world that day, he added. It was the Pope and the Second Vatican Council and the Roman Catholic Church, which had broken through the Iron Curtain with its message of peace. Not only had Soviet Premier Khrushchev been given a new view of the Church, her moral authority and her inner vitality; the whole world was suddenly aware of the Church and her message. The Church was suddenly very relevant and very necessary.

If this Council Father was right, and everything indicated that he was, the messages between Rome and Moscow were not simply the result of Communist propaganda, nor simply the result of the Holy Father's seeking to improve conditions for the faithful in the Church of Silence. The context was one of impending nuclear disaster and, amid the darkness, the light of Christ's Church streaming from the Second Vatican Council's work of renewal. To His Holiness Pope John XXIII and the Second Vatican Council, the whole human race owes a great debt of gratitude.